Embodied Research Through Music Composition and Evocative Life-Writing

Embodied Research Through Music Composition and Evocative Life-Writing: Disrupting Diaspora examines how attendance to the lived experience of diaspora can impact our scholarly understanding of the term.

Through the entanglements between her life and practice as a music composer, British Iranian author Soosan Lolavar weaves together a uniquely embodied approach to academic discussions, enriched by both her personal narrative and music. This book powerfully argues for the unique contribution of ways of knowing that are palpably understood through the body. Lolavar scrutinises the ways that the metaphor of diaspora has left indelible marks on her life and work, exploring these through the narrative presented in this book and publically available recordings of her music. This process allows her to construct new theoretical conceptions of diaspora which bring nuance and detail to a concept used widely across the humanities and social sciences. *Disrupting Diaspora* presents a map for transdisciplinary work which triangulates artistic practice, theory and evocative life-writing in lively and reflexive ways. In so doing, it contributes to a growing field of embodied scholarly work.

This book is primarily written for an academic audience with interests in embodied research methods, diaspora studies, practice-as-research in general and creative research in music composition in particular. It will be suitable for students in the disciplines of music studies, music composition, sociology, communications, creative writing, anthropology and human geography.

Soosan Lolavar is a musician, lecturer and researcher. She lives and works in London, UK, and her music has been performed across the world.

Embodied Research Through Music Composition and Evocative Life-Writing

Disrupting Diaspora

Soosan Lolavar

Routledge
Taylor & Francis Group

LONDON AND NEW YORK

First published 2024
by Routledge
4 Park Square, Milton Park, Abingdon, Oxon OX14 4RN

and by Routledge
605 Third Avenue, New York, NY 10158

*Routledge is an imprint of the Taylor & Francis Group,
an informa business*

British Library Cataloguing-in-Publication Data
A catalogue record for this book is available from the British Library

ISBN: 978-1-032-39804-4 (hbk)
ISBN: 978-1-032-39805-1 (pbk)
ISBN: 978-1-003-35145-0 (ebk)

DOI: 10.4324/9781003351450

Typeset in Optima
by Apex CoVantage, LLC

Contents

Acknowledgements

There are many people to thank for their help over the many years of this complex project.

Many of the ideas contained in this book started life as part of a PhD in music at City, University of London (2016–2021). In this period, Rachel Stratton and Harry Pearse offered sage advice on the trials of doing a PhD as well a sympathetic ear when everything was going wrong. Katherine Waters was a voice of such calm and kindness throughout and edited a version of the section on *I Am the Spring, You Are the Earth* printed here. Dominic Murcott was a constant source of support, consistently encouraging me to believe in myself and my project.

My deep gratitude goes to my whole supervisory team of Laudan Nooshin, Tullis Rennie and Newton Armstrong for their help and guidance over the years. There were some highs and lows, but time has allowed me to reflect on the great generosity you all showed in supporting my project. This book would not exist without each of your expertise.

Thank you to Jasmine Ulmer and James Salvo for believing in me to write this book. I have never worked with kinder people and am so grateful for your constant support and unending patience!

Particular thanks go to Rachel Beckles Willson and Joe Browning who acted as my PhD examiners in 2021. Experiencing a viva in absentia while undergoing treatment for cancer was not the ending to the PhD journey I was expecting, but your thoughtful and encouraging report more than made up for this strange sense of dislocation. Your support of my work has been invaluable, and your hugely generous comments on the draft of the manuscript proved instrumental in refining my argument.

Finally, all thanks go to Will and my family, without whom much of my work would not exist.

Preface

Some of my earliest memories of Iran are not really memories at all. At least, I cannot be sure if my recollections are real events or, rather, inventions fashioned out of half-remembered fragments and shot through with my own anxieties. Early trips to Tehran remain like faded family photographs in my mind. While I can make out the outline of people's features, I can never quite discern their expressions, their faces blurred by linguistic and cultural barriers that left me feeling like an outsider for many decades. Perhaps I find it so difficult to remember my early visits to Iran because those times are shrouded in such a sense of confusion and dislocation. As a child of Iranian and British heritage with a parent from each country, I have spent many years grappling with my peculiar identity, constantly asking questions about who or what I am.

I was born in the UK in the late 1980s. My father was unusual amongst Iranians living outside Iran because he did not come to the UK as a result of the 1979 revolution. In fact, he moved to the UK much earlier in 1964 at the age of 15. He was sent to a boarding school in the north of England, alone, with the aim of learning English and eventually becoming a doctor. The plan was always that he would return to Iran and enrich the family with his "international" education and command of an important foreign language, but as is often the case, things did not work out that way. In the mid-1970s, he met my mother, and by the end of the decade, they were married and living in London (notwithstanding a brief period after the revolution when they tried to live in Iran).

I grew up projecting an outwardly uncomplicated Britishness at the same time as engaging in an almost constant process of negotiation between my two cultures. For well over a decade, I would finish a week of British schooling and then attend an Iranian community group on Saturdays where I purported to learn Farsi (with little success) but, more importantly, met other British Iranian children and learnt about Iranian food, culture and dance. The lines of discipline and behaviour in my family were often confusing, sometimes drawn in ways commensurate with friends at my overwhelmingly white British school, at others totally alien to that which I experienced in wider society. I gradually deduced that my Iranianness had to be hidden from the outside world as it was strange and foreign and would surely be rejected by others. At the same time, I was in constant trouble at home for behaving in ways that – it was explained to me – stood outside the norms of an Iranian childhood. I developed a sense of myself as a constant failure – too Iranian for my British life, too British within my Iranian community – and became an obsessive perfectionist in all other areas to hide this ultimate truth. Much like Amal Treacher's (2000: 102) highly personal account of managing relationships with her Egyptian father and British mother, I struggled with "my anger at the strain of having to fit in and my continual and pervasive feeling that I am not the right thing."

This book explores the lifetime impact of such issues. Specifically, it considers my experiences of double-consciousness, an internalised form of subject-object dualism in which the individual looks upon themself through the eyes of a dominant, hostile culture. Double-consciousness is a term coined by African American theorist W.E.B. Du Bois (1994) which has enabled me to make sense of the deeply embedded sense of dislocation I have experienced my whole life. It has allowed me to theorise a sense of myself as fractured between two polarised identities which I label British and Iranian. My experiences of double-consciousness caused me to conceive of Iranianness as something external to me for many years. In this way, an important part of my lived experience remained ambivalent and unfulfilled, separating me from a sense of myself and also from my Iranian father.

Double-consciousness is fundamentally based on the assumed essential paradox between the dominant culture (in my case, British) and the subaltern form (Iranian). Within this framework, to be Iranian is to be fundamentally Other and suspicious; double-consciousness describes the mechanism by which I, as a British Iranian woman, launch these feelings of distrust against myself. In this book, I will consider whether the metaphor of diaspora – which offers an emancipatory and emergent model of identity based on multi-locationality and syncretism (Gilroy, 1993; Hall, 1990; Clifford, 1994) – can help reconcile the sense of dislocation I have felt for many years. Through an intensely personal, embodied and material process of grappling with these concepts, my work aims to add crucial experiential dimension to theoretical discussion of diaspora, a term which continues to have major relevance across the humanities and social sciences.

Crucially, this book not only adds to our conception of diaspora but also makes the case for the unique contribution of creative arts practice to scholarly discourse. Despite rapid growth in recent years, arts-based research remains niche and underfunded in most contexts. As I aim to show, this way of working critically subverts the dominance of a research model based on detached analysis performed by a singular human subject. Through the use of practice-based models, my account prioritises physical engagement with materials and therefore recognises the fundamentally performative nature of all knowledge-producing practices. In turn, this approach develops methodologies for the assessment and dissemination of practice-based knowledge in notated instrumental music – a kind of work which sadly remains highly specialised with little broader impact. By using practice-based work in music composition to reflect deeply on the theoretical construction of diaspora, my work also pushes against a tendency for music to be considered largely as the *output* of diasporic encounters rather than as a way of knowing that could bring new insight to this term. In this way, my account challenges a number of scholarly and disciplinary agendas at once.

Specifically, in this book, I explore two of my own music compositions – *Tradition-Hybrid-Survival* and *I Am the Spring, You Are the Earth* – in order to grapple with the concepts of both double-consciousness and diaspora. While some commentators (Gilroy, 1993; Hall, 1990; Clifford, 1994) suggest that diaspora offers an emancipatory model of identity, I argue that this is not enough to facilitate a reconciliation of double-consciousness as I experience it. This is particularly relevant in those cases when diaspora deals in framings of place and travel that align with the concept of "transport," a metaphor for travel developed by Ingold (2007, 2008), which I will explore in more detail in Chapter 4. As I will explain, "transport" constructs place as a series of defined and delineated locations between which the body of the passenger is passively transported, and when diaspora reproduces such a framing of place and travel, the binary fragmentations of double-consciousness are reasserted. In contrast, a concept of travel and place based on "wayfaring" – in which all travel is a dynamic process of moving along trails – makes space for a form of diaspora through which a reconciliation of double-consciousness becomes possible.

These findings are intimately tied to the processes of conceiving, composing, reflecting on and analysing my compositions through an intertwined methodology of music composition and evocative life-writing. This way of working yields insights that would not be possible using more standard means of detached observation alone. In this way, my work stands apart from much scholarship on diaspora in the field of music studies – both academic scholarship analysing the links between music and diaspora on the one hand and arts research which lacks critical commentary on the other. In contrast, my project will engage music composition and evocative life-writing specifically as a means for problematising theories of diaspora, developing a means by which performative methods in general and notated instrumental composition in particular can contribute to broader theory.

These various aims are achieved through the use of a tripartite methodology that moves back and forth between analytical knowledge (theory), practice (music composition) and experiential knowledge (evocative life-writing). This means that the personal and lifelong impact of double-consciousness is manifested in the relationships set in motion in various music compositions, and subsequent analysis of these works brings to the surface aspects of personal experience that might not otherwise have been accessible. These processes both guide and are guided by evocative forms of writing which connect personal experience to broader political, social and critical concerns. Moreover, both methods continually reflect back on theory, adding nuance to our conceptualisation of diaspora as a term with broad applicability. The ambitious and wide-ranging aims of this project are set against an intimate and personal focus. While I aim to disrupt a number of agendas in scholarly work across a range of disciplines, I do not lose sight of the fact that I work towards these aims through deep, reflective consideration of my life and music. Such processes occur against the backdrop of many decades of complex experiences in respect of my Iranianness and ongoing attempts to construct a sense of myself that is whole and singular.

Alongside this written form of my argument, I strongly encourage the reader to listen to recordings of the two pieces which are central to my analysis – *Tradition-Hybrid-Survival* and *I Am the Spring, You Are the Earth*. The discussion contained in this book tells only part of the story, and it is only through combining this with experience of the sounding music that my argument can be fully grasped. *Tradition-Hybrid-Survival* can be accessed through the album *Girl* recorded by Ruthless Jabiru, conducted by Kelly Lovelady and released on the record label Nonclassical in 2024. *I Am the Spring, You Are the Earth* can be found on the album *Stepping Back, Jumping In* by Laura Jurd which was released on Edition Records in 2019.

1 Disrupting Agendas

From a young age, I understood a number of facts about myself: first, that my dual identity rendered me an outsider who didn't really fit in anywhere, and second, that it was only through intense self-management that I would have any hope of surviving this situation. Born in London with one parent from Iran and one from the UK, my early life was defined by constant movement between an Iranian diaspora community, friends in London who were overwhelmingly white and an extended Iranian family living in Iran. These worlds were all intensely different, and each demanded a new version of me that I presented faithfully. I developed impressive skills in hyper-vigilance and code-switching such that, as Anzaldúa (2012: 60) put it, I was "excruciatingly alive to the world," with a unique capacity to sense the environment and present the required version of myself.

Crucially, however, this sensing was largely tied up in acts of concealment and self-sabotage. I cannot remember a time before I "knew" that being Iranian made you strange and foreign. I grew up in the 1980–90s, not long after the Iranian revolution (1979) and ensuing hostage crisis (1979–81), both of which preceded the long and painful Iran-Iraq war (1980–88), about which Nobel Peace Prize winner Henry Kissinger famously said, "It's a shame there can only be one loser." Images of Iran on British television in this period were exclusively defined by Islamic fanaticism, violence and presumed barbarity. (I cannot say the situation is wholly different while writing this in 2023.) I absorbed this material and understood the need to distance myself from it. Through constant vigilance, I was able to present an uncomplicated sense of Britishness to the wider world without ever explicitly denying my Iranianness.

This masquerade would all come crashing down if people met my father and assumed (as I *knew* they would) that he was just another dangerous Iranian like the kind they had seen on the news. I was terrified that people might abuse or mock him, and I knew that observing this humiliation would be too much for me to bear. I was also scared that he

DOI: 10.4324/9781003351450-1

would out me as the foreigner I really was. And so, I kept us both safe by pushing him and his foreign body to the edge of my life for many years.

While I exhausted myself trying to present an image of uncompli-cated Britishness, I also felt fundamentally rejected by aspects of the Iranian (diaspora) community. This was perhaps unsurprising since I had fostered such a strong sense of dislocation from both my Iranian self and my Iranian father for many years. I was constantly called "not a real Iranian" by members of our community. Sometimes this was delivered in jest or even as a compliment; at others it was indicative of an undercur-rent of ethno-nationalism in Iranian culture which reproduces a singular image of Iranian identity. In any case, I believe a crucial backdrop to all such comments was the idea that Otherness was central to the Iranian diaspora experience in the UK, and due to my passing privilege, I could never be fully considered Iranian in a true sense. I began to experience my Iranianness as a thing that stood outside me whose legitimacy could only be affirmed by other people.

For many years, I felt trapped between two worlds: suppressing my foreignness in wider British society at the same time as being labelled "not a real Iranian" by some members of my own community. The es-sential backdrop to this is a British society in which to be Iranian is to be fundamentally Other, strange, foreign and dangerous. This denigra-tion of the subaltern form led me to suppress my Iranian self while this same mechanism (and the effectiveness of my self-presentation as "not-Other") lay behind my experience of rejection by some diaspora mem-bers. I struggled to construct a sense of myself that accounted for my dual heritage and soon began to experience the dislocations of double-consciousness – the pain of embodying two opposing ideals within one human self. This caused me to experience Iranianness as an external and objective "thing" that was at once ambivalent, dangerous and unfulfilled.

It was in my 20s after years of working as a composer when I began to turn to music to explore my Iranianness further. After several years spent formally and informally studying Iranian classical music, I began to weave ideas drawn from this musical tradition into my broader training as a composer. Thus, I wrote a large work for Iranian and western instru-ments (*Only Sound Remains*, 2014), drew on Iranian rhythmic cycles as the basis for a piece for symphony orchestra (*Set Your Life on Fire*, 2015) and made use of Iranian folk songs as source material (*Girl*, 2017). This work was easily positioned in a kind of east-meets-west paradigm which gained both media attention and support from funding organisations ea-ger to make a well-meaning point about hybridity and multiculturalism in the UK.

After the initial excitement of discovering a new musical repository from which to draw ideas, I started to consider whether mining my own ethnic-ity for artistic inspiration was such a good idea. Perhaps I was exoticising myself, maybe even taking part in my own self-Othering. It caused me to wonder whether I had ever really stopped my practice of code-switching. Now I was merely playing the part of the perfect hybrid artist whose work found increasing recognition in the UK as part of a left-leaning attempt to "respond" to events like the US Muslim ban (2016) and unending wars in the Middle East. My hybridity meant I was safe and unthreatening in the context of the UK; my work found success as part of what Winegar (2008) refers to as a western predilection for Middle Eastern art that circumvents contemporary Islam.

Despite these misgivings, it was clear that my work with Iranian music was exciting, vital and important to my practice. And yet, I was keen to move beyond a fairly basic version of hybridity based on fixed, binary relations between white cultural forms and a non-white, exotic Other (Taylor, 2007: 156–7). Over years of work I was able to refine my practice, moving away from music dealing in a fixed version of Otherness and towards something more complex, productive and defined largely by itself.

It is part of this period of growth and discovery that is documented here. In this book, I narrate the process by which I engage music composition and evocative life-writing in order to confront and reconcile my experiences of double-consciousness. This process has been rich and productive, helping heal a major fissure in my life and affecting a great personal healing. At the same time, I consider my work relevant to a variety of scholarly positions in the social sciences, humanities and disciplines of arts research. Indeed, just as my work has disrupted a number of patterns and tendencies in my personal life, I am aware of the ways that it pushes against a number of important agendas that exist in much contemporary scholarship. These areas of disruption also form some of the key aims of this book, which can be defined as follows:

1 Problematising the dominance of a research agenda based on detached analysis, instead prioritising methods of physical engagement with materials which are grounded in enactivism;
2 Arguing the case for music practice adding nuance and detail to our understanding of diaspora; and
3 Responding to the growing call for work which develops methodologies for assessing and communicating practice-derived knowledge in music.

(Leedham and Scheuregger, 2020; Pace,
2016; Doğantan-Dack, 2015)

In this chapter, I will deal with each of these issues in turn. Thus, in the section entitled "Thinking and Doing," I will sketch out the landscape of dominant research agendas and make the case for embodied approaches. Next, in "Adding Nuance to Diaspora Through Creative Arts Practice,"

I will consider how performative approaches play an essential role in exploring embodied experiences of Otherness and are crucial to a more nuanced understanding of diaspora. Finally, in "The Absence of Music Composition from Interdisciplinary Arts Practice," I will consider the lack of practice-as-research methodologies in music in general and notated instrumental music in particular, in preparation for a discussion of my response to this situation in Chapter 2.

Thinking and Doing

In *How to Do Things with Words* (1975), Austin describes the difference between constative speech utterances which describe or report on the world and performative statements in which "the issuing of an utterance is the performance of an action" (Austin, 1975: 6). Austin gives examples of the "I do" spoken at a wedding or a judge's statement "I sentence you to five years in prison" as exemplifying "the power of speech acts to have real effects in the world" (Bolt, 2016: 133). Barbara Bolt uses Austin's framework of performative and constative utterances to delineate the essential differences between research-as-science and research-as-creative practice. As she describes it, research-as-science[1] is aligned more with the constative model of speech since it is based on describing, recording, analysing and contemplating, while art-as-research tends towards the principle of performative utterances since it is based on forms of practical involvement with materials. She uses as a shorthand for these two methods: the terms "thinking" and "doing" (Bolt, 2016: 137).

Following Foucault (1980), we might remind ourselves that "a research agenda" is really a particular kind of discursive practice which "constrains and enables what can be said . . . [and] define[s] what counts as meaningful statements" (Barad, 2007: 146). These statements differ across time and space and are under constant development through ongoing processes of "writing back," which challenge previous norms and ideals. While neither static nor hegemonic, varied research agendas certainly function within academe to constrain and enable particular kinds of work. Against this backdrop, Bolt's use of the term "thinking" reflects a model of mainstream qualitative and quantitative research which is built on a perception of the singular human subject as separate from a pre-formed and enclosed environment. This model assumes that the "thinking" human subject periodically steps outside the world in order to observe and analyse it from a distance. The issue with this framework is that there is simply no process of "thinking" that is separable from or disentangled from notions of "doing." As Karen Barad puts it "knowing does not comes from standing at a distance and representing but rather from a *direct material engagement with the world*" (Barad, 2007: 49, original emphasis). Therefore, any attempt to consider or explore our environment will always involve physical engagement with the material world of which we are intrinsically a part.

These ideas are summed up by the enactivist model which shows us that all mental content derives from physical interaction with the world (Cole, 2017: 59). As Varela et al. describe it:

> We propose as a name the term enactive to emphasise the growing conviction that cognition is not the representation of a pre-given world by a pre-given mind but is rather the enactment of a world and a mind on the basis of a history of the variety of actions that a being in the world performs.
>
> (Varela et al., 1991: 9)

That is to say, "doing" and "thinking" cannot be clearly separated because subject and world are always intimately intertwined and, further, because physical engagement with the world is the *fundamental* basis of cognition and experience. Thus, all experience is essentially performative in nature because, as Krueger describes it, "*body shapes mind*" (Krueger, 2009: 100, emphasis in original), or, to put it another way, all thinking is fundamentally rooted in doing.

The enactivist model is further developed by Karen Barad, whose work demonstrates the way that all seemingly cognitive processes are fundamentally rooted in bodily action. She illustrates this point by describing the functioning of the scanning tunnelling microscope (STM), a machine we might think of as enabling us to "see" things on the level of single atoms (Barad, 2007: 52–3). Barad explains how image formation using an STM is closer to a process of touch than a process of sight. This is because the content of the image is *produced* through intervention and material engagement, rather than merely *observed* through detached, transcendent means.

In order to produce an image, the STM manoeuvres a microscopic tip (the point of which is the size of a single atom) across the surface of the specimen much like a blind person uses their cane to determine the topography of an environment. Furthermore, the STM operator must carry out a huge number of highly skilled practical tasks – including preparing the specimen; cutting a new tip; adjusting the specimen's tilt coordinates; isolating the specimen from light, vibrations, air currents and temperature fluctuations; and ultimately deciding if the image produced is a "good image" – all of which bear on the success or failure of the "seeing" the STM facilitates. As a result, the STM does not merely magnify or represent a pre-existing reality but, rather, produces images which are "condensations or traces of multiple practical engagements" (Barad, 2007: 53). Thus, in contrast to a constative (returning here to Austin's term) model which posits that there exist ontological realities on the one hand and our representations of them on the other (Barad,

2007: 46), a performative model posits that all practices that produce knowledge are a matter of intervening rather than representing, and *"theorizing, like experimenting, is a material practice"* (Barad, 2007: 55, emphasis in original).

Of course, there has been a wide variety of scholarly work over several decades exploring embodiment and bodily experience and which therefore attends to the performative model of knowledge production outlined previously (Merleau-Ponty, 1962; Pillow, 2001; Spry, 2001). As Pink (2015: 13ff) outlines, we might observe how research in the field of geography has: decentered the sense of sight as the primary form of knowledge acquisition (Porteous, 1990), recognised the ways that human experience of the environment derived through the senses plays a role in structuring space and place (Rodaway, 1994) and argued for the conceptualisation of space through a sensorial paradigm (Thrift, 2006). In sociology some key work has advanced the cause of auditory epistemology through an analysis of everyday personal stereo usage (Bull, 2000), explored the role of intercorporeal knowledge amongst members of an anaesthetic team in a teaching hospital (Hindmarsh and Pilnick, 2007) or called for a multi-sensory approach to sociology in order to enable new kinds of critical imagination (Back and Puwar, 2012).

Despite this growing area of work, constative research-as-science (or disembodied "thinking") remains the "'model' par excellence" of academia (Bolt, 2016: 137). While the relative proliferation of practice-as-research in recent decades stands as an important example of the capacity for change within research agendas, the fact that the British Academy (one of the two major funding bodies for post-doctoral research in the arts and humanities in the UK) continues to view arts research as outside its remit at the time of writing suggests the continued primacy of approaches which shore up the model of detached, deliberative research methods.

Against this backdrop, it is so-called performative methods (and particularly evocative life-writing and music composition) which are the essential focus of this book. Crucially, however, I do not suggest that academia should eschew those epistemologies that tend towards empirical, distanced analysis in favour of those which prioritise experiential, embodied knowledge and active engagement with materials. Critics might suggest that this represents a kind of nativist turn wherein the unquestioning "authority of experience" supersedes all other kinds of knowledge claims (see Fuss, 1989). This merely replaces one hierarchy – positivism – with another – essentialism. Rather, my argument is that analytical and observational epistemologies are never actually detached and objective. The transcendent empiricism of the world which is idealised in mainstream qualitative and quantitative research overlooks a crucial facet of knowledge of ourselves and our environment. Indeed, all knowledge-producing practices are materially engaged means of research in the world since there is no means by which the human (or non-human) subject can step outside the world in order to analyse and observe it.

It would be wrong to suggest that this books eschews all styles of writing which tend towards the analytical and deliberative. Examples of these can be found especially in Chapter 3, where I discuss in detail the concepts of double-consciousness and diaspora. Part of this text unveils a more standard scholarly narrative in which various viewpoints on these concepts are explored and weighed against each other. Crucially, however, I intertwine this way of thinking with more embodied, performative narratives, combining a scholarly view of these concepts with my own personal experience of such terms. This aims to highlight the essentially performative nature of all analytical knowledge since there is no detached, transcendent observation of either double-consciousness or diaspora that stands outside our intimate physical engagement with the world from which these terms derive.

The enactivist model (Varela et al., 1991: 9) is an established paradigm for thinking through knowledge-producing practices which has had significant impact on scholarly thought for some time. The aim of my project is specifically to bring the enactivist approach to bear on musical practice in notated instrumental music (explored through evocative life-writing) in order to explore discourses of diaspora. In fact, it is to the concept of diaspora which I now turn in order to consider how an approach which engages with creative arts practice can add crucial nuance and detail to this term.

Adding Nuance to Diaspora Through Creative Arts Practice

On a muggy September evening our taxi lurched agonisingly forwards through one of Tehran's ever-present traffic jams, gradually edging us closer to the Ministry of Interior building where a huge crowd had already formed outside. I was anxious about missing the start of the concert (scheduled for 9pm and my watch now reading 8:57pm) but then remembered that this was Iran; concerts very rarely started on time.

Hundreds of people were gathered on the pavement outside the building. Old couples, families and music students carrying instruments all chatted animatedly in groups, casually spilling out on to the main road causing even more traffic chaos. Nobody seemed particularly bothered by such a commotion, and the excitement for the forthcoming concert was palpable. Men and women filed into separate, gender-segregated lines for the inevitable bag checks that come with government buildings and gradually made their way inside the large concert hall. Just before the concert began, at 9.25pm, there was a commotion in the front row, and the crowd burst into spontaneous applause and a standing ovation. Mohammad Javad Zarif – the Foreign Minister and key architect of the landmark nuclear deal – turned to the crowd and bowed. Shortly after, Kayhan Kalhor – the kamancheh player and world-renowned proponent of Iranian and Kurdish music – entered to huge applause alongside the Rembrandt Trio, a Dutch jazz ensemble.

(Fieldnotes, March 2017)[2]

As is often the case in both creative and scholarly work, this project started out as something quite different. In 2016, I began my PhD in music at City, University of London with an intention of exploring the emerging genre of *musiqi-ye talfighi* (fusion music), a term used in Iran to refer to music across a range of genres that combines influences from distinct sources. I was particularly interested in those artists combining ideas from Iranian and western art music.

In 2017, I travelled to Iran a number of times, attending festivals of new music, interviewing composers and performers and generally immersing myself in the scene. I soon found myself professionally entangled with many of the musicians I met. In fact, one of the pieces I analyse in this book (*Tradition-Hybrid-Survival*) was commissioned by conductor Kaveh Mirhosseini and was to be premiered by his Cantus Ensemble at Roudaki Hall in Tehran. Sadly, due to the ongoing precarity of life in Iran, our commission agreement didn't quite work out as planned and the premier never took place. The piece received its first performance in London instead.

I found this period of early PhD research in Iran extremely stressful. I suffered with almost constant anxiety, worrying about what I wore, my language skills, balancing time with my family in Iran and my interlocutors, whether I was writing sufficient fieldnotes and generally that my whole project would end in failure. I have no doubt such feelings are common for most ethnographers, but amongst all this there was a nagging feeling of a deeper kind of failure. I felt instinctively that *I should be better at this because I'm supposed to be Iranian.* And the fact that I was struggling seemed to prove to me that my identity was a sham after all. One of the worst days of my research was when I was sitting with a visiting Polish woman, and a nearby Iranian musician referred to us as "the two foreigners." I remember my face going red hot with embarrassment. Of course, what he said makes perfect sense; I was born in the UK. But this easy dismissal of my Iranian identity opened up a wound inside me that had lain raw since childhood and confirmed the fact that I just didn't fit in.

Not long after the visit described here, what seemed like a burgeoning new relationship of openness between Iran and the west suddenly changed dramatically. The British government advised against all but essential travel to Iran, my university said they would not insure me if I chose to go, and close friends who had always gone back and forth postponed planned trips. Initially, I struggled on and tried to complete my ethnography online, but it wasn't long before I was forced to rethink my plans for my PhD entirely. After a great deal of thought, I decided to turn inwards and focus on my own practice as a composer.

After deciding to refocus my PhD to an exploration of my own music and its relation to the genre of *musiqi-ye talfighi*, it soon became clear to me that there was something interesting going on in the music I had written during this period. When looking deeply at my creative work, I could see that my complex experiences of diaspora were clearly audible. Perhaps this is not surprising – artists regularly use their practice as a means for responding to their life experiences. What was more interesting to me was the way that delving deeper into my music, at the same time as considering this work against the backdrop of my life experiences, opened up an analytical space where I could question and reconsider diaspora – and my relationship to it – on a theoretical level. It was not merely a case of writing music about my experience of diaspora but, rather, of music composition acting as an epistemology that provided new insights into diaspora and my relationship to it.

It is by drawing on these experiences and others that I have constructed the main arguments of this book: namely, that art-based work has a unique capacity to confront the psychic and emotional experiences of Otherness and dislocation which can form a central part of diasporic experience. This is because of the way that both arts practice and Otherness are explicitly performative in nature, which is to say that they are ways of knowing which are palpably felt and experienced through the body. As we have seen, Bolt's (2016) model defines arts research as being concerned with practical engagement with materials. Ingold has taken this further and shown that the relationship between maker and materials – artist and medium – is fundamentally based on ongoing correspondence. As he puts it:

> I want to think of making . . . as a process of *growth*. This is to place the maker from the outset as a participant in amongst a world of active materials.
>
> (Ingold, 2013: 21, emphasis in original)

Making is thus a cyclical and embodied relationship between artisan and material. Central to Ingold's argument is Gibson's (1979) concept of affordance "which emphasizes the reciprocal relationship between a perceiving organism and its environment" (Clarke, 2010: 106). This concept has been employed by Clarke (2005) in his ecological approach to the perception of musical meaning, which considers perception and action as interdependent. As he describes it, "to a human being a chair affords sitting on, while to a termite it affords eating. Equally the same chair affords use as a weapon to a human being who needs one" (Clarke, 2010: 106). Thus, the relationship between organism and environment is dialectical, "neither simply a case of perceivers imposing their needs on an indifferent environment, nor a fixed environment determining possibilities" (Clarke, 2010: 107). Similarly, making is a material and embodied process by which maker and material, artist and environment, "join forces" (Ingold, 2013: 21) and act together. Materials are non-static; they each represent "one path or trajectory through a maze of trajectories" (Ingold, 2013: 31), and the maker plays a key role in opening up or closing down possible routes. In essence, the maker *follows* the flow of materials (Deleuze and Guattari, 2004: 450–1 in Ingold, 2013: 25) by moving with and amongst them.

Against this backdrop of performative models of embodied making, we might consider how the experience of Otherness is similarly expressed through the body. Indeed, there is a long history of work by feminists, writers of colour, disabled writers and many others which presents embodied accounts of the experience of non-normative subjectivity. As hooks describes it, "suffering [is] . . . a way of knowing that is often expressed through the body . . . This complexity of experience can rarely be voiced and named from a distance" (hooks, 1991: 182–3).[3]

An early and central example of writing exploring the embodied nature of experiences of Otherness is the 1903 work, *The Souls of Black Folk* (1994) by W.E.B. Du Bois, in which he sets out his theory of double-consciousness. I will explore the details of Du Bois' argument in Chapter 3. At this point, it is useful to consider the ways in which Du Bois drew on his own embodied experience of racial oppression in the United States to construct an argument which presents a theoretical means of understanding Otherness. As Ciccariello-Maher (2009: 373) explains, Du Bois's concept of the veil – a metaphor for racial oppression – forms out of a personal experience of rejection in his childhood when a new female student refuses a gift from him "peremptorily, with a glance," a small gesture but one which lays bare for him his positioning in a racist society. In this one moment, Du Bois is confronted with the life-changing fact that he is "shut out from their world by a vast veil" (Du Bois, 1994: 2), and it is this realisation – subsequently analysed – which opens the door for the development of his theory of double-consciousness. What is important about Du Bois's account is that his seminal theorisation of the psychic effects of racism is built not from an attempt at detached and transcendent observation but, rather, from deep reflection on the emotional effects of his personal experiences. It is this embodied experience of suffering, subsequently analysed, which paves the way for significant theoretical insight.

Du Bois's theorisation of the psychic and emotional conflicts unleashed by racism is also crucial to the work of Frantz Fanon. His 1952 work *Black Skin, White Masks* (2008) is another example of a fundamentally personal account which helps theorise the experience of Otherness. In this book, Fanon accounts for the inferiority complex inculcated by processes of colonialism with reference to his own personal struggles. As he puts it, "As I begin to recognize that the Negro is the symbol of sin, I catch myself hating the Negro. But then I recognize that I am a Negro" (Fanon, 2008: 153). As Ziauddin Sardar notes in the forward to the 2008 edition, "The text changes and unfolds itself as the experiences of the author transform and change him, as he suffocates, gasps, twists, struggles" (Sardar in Fanon, 2008: xii). That is to say, the physical, embodied effects of racism are foregrounded, and it is from this way of knowing that theoretical insight emerges. His writing unfolds in such a way that theory is *formed* and *shaped* by his bodily experience, not the other way round.

The texts mentioned here share an essential quality with the fundamentals of arts practice since they are both deeply embodied ways of knowing felt and expressed through the body. By combining such approaches, we have the potential to unveil new insights about diaspora, highlighting the embodied experiences of Otherness and dislocation which are often missing from accounts which tend towards the constative pole of research. It is against this backdrop that my own project emerges. As I will explore further in subsequent chapters, my experience of diaspora is inherently entangled with questions of Otherness which find their apotheosis in the psychic state of double-consciousness. I explore this state through methods of both evocative life-writing and music composition with the aim of bringing new and important nuance to our theorisation of diaspora.

The Absence of Music Composition From Interdisciplinary Arts Practice

Before considering the relative absence of music composition from a growing body of work developing methodologies for practice-derived knowledge, it may first be beneficial to delineate some of the different sub-disciplines within the broader field of music studies. For the sake of ease, we can somewhat simplistically divide the study of music into largely "academic" and largely "practice-based" research. Within the "academic" branch, some of the main areas include musicology, ethnomusicology and sociology of music. By contrast, "practice-based" work tends to take the form of music composition (writing/creating new music) and/or performance (performing, interpreting and creating music). Obviously, this is a very crude model, and there are innumerable examples of work which functions between or across such sub-disciplines or rejects them completely. For reference, I myself tend to operate across the sub-disciplines of music composition, musicology, ethnomusicology and sociology of music. Within the sub-discipline of music composition there is, of course, a huge variety of work, but two areas that are pertinent to my discussion are the field of notated instrumental composition (where my work sits) on the one hand and acousmatic approaches, which include soundscapes, soundwalks and field recordings, on the other.

Against the backdrop of this model, Practice-based research in music is conspicuous by its absence from many of the major publications advancing the cause of interdisciplinary arts research. It is unrepresented in either *Carnal Knowledge: Towards a New Materialism Through the Arts* (Barrett and Bolt, 2013) or *Material Inventions: Applying Creative Arts Research* (Barrett and Bolt, 2014) and has a cursory mention in both *Teaching Artistic Research: Conversations Across Cultures* (Mateus-Berr and Jochum, 2020) and *Beyond Text: Learning Through Arts-Based Research* (Adams and Owens, 2021). As Pace (2016: 63, footnote 8) points out, it does not feature in *Practice as Research: Approaches to Creative Arts Enquiry* (Barrett and Bolt, 2010) and is only briefly mentioned in *Practice as Research in the Arts* (Nelson, 2013). Notwithstanding publications with a specific focus on music,[4] this absence is symptomatic of a general isolation of music from broader discussions of arts practice. This is in part explained by the way that the discipline of music has lagged behind other fields in developing methodologies which allow for the assessment and communication of practice-derived knowledge (Leedham and Scheuregger, 2020: 66).

As Leedham and Scheuregger (2020: 66) point out, music composition "stumbled somewhat accidentally into the P-R [practice-research] camp" in such a way that "its sense of methodological coherence is the least clear amongst P-R disciplines." This has led to a situation in which music composers are *still* hashing out the debate over whether or not their discipline constitutes a form of research at a time when other disciplines have moved beyond such discussions (Leedham and Scheuregger, 2020: 66). The oppositional nature of such debates is exemplified by Croft's (2015: 6) claim that "there are, by and large, two kinds of composers in academia today – those who labour under the delusion that they are doing a kind of 'research,' and those who recognise the absurdity of this idea." (See Pace, 2016 and Reeves, 2016 for counterarguments.)

In those interdisciplinary publications in which music does feature as part of a broader discussion of practice-as-research, it is often acousmatic approaches to sound which are represented, to the relative absence of notated compositional approaches. For example, *Doing Sensory Ethnography* (Pink, 2015: 173) features a discussion of soundscape composition with no mention of other kinds of music. *The Body in Sound, Music and Performance* (O'Keefe and Nogueira, 2022) discusses only acousmatic approaches to music composition. *Method Meets Art: Art-Based Research Practice* (Leavy, 2009) features a whole chapter on music without any discussion of notation or instrumentation, instead focusing on sound-based practices alongside music as metaphor or a way of collecting and representing data. As a result of this general state of omission, discussion of notated instrumental music has little interdisciplinary impact and remains siloed within specialised music departments. The greater interdisciplinary representation of acousmatic approaches to music is connected more broadly to the ways that the field of sound art defines itself. Brandon LaBelle, one of the key scholars of sound art, quotes John Cage in order to make clear the distinction between his conception of embodied sound art on the one hand and the disembodied "classical tradition" on the other:

> The experimental ethos as exemplified by Cage refutes the classical tradition, for "traditional dialectical music is representational." . . . In contrast, the new experimentalism calls . . . "for a new form of mental collaboration with the music" in which "the singularity of the moment" comes into being "in the listener's ear."
>
> (LaBelle, 2015: 7; quoting John Cage in Chanan, 1994: 273–4)

Here, LaBelle defines traditional music as merely representational, an objective form that exists outside human engagement. In contrast, sound art is considered inherently embodied since it is produced *in collaboration* with the listener and, in fact, only comes into being in direct relationship with the body itself. He further explains:

> By overturning the musical object so as to insert the presence of the listener, Cage resituates the terms by which the referent of music takes on social weight, beyond symbolic systems and toward immediacy and the profound presence of being there.
>
> (LaBelle, 2015: 7–8)

If sound art moves beyond objecthood because of the way it is so closely intertwined with the embodied listener, then, as LaBelle argues, this kind of composition defines itself as inherently more immediate, more situated and more social than more traditional kinds of music. Further, the definition of a soundscape tends to put concepts of environmental emplacement, perception and cultural meaning at its centre. As Drever (2002: 21–2) points out, the *Handbook for Acoustic Ecology* (1999) defines a "soundscape" as "an environment of sound (or sonic environment) with emphasis on the way it is perceived and understood by an individual, or by a society" (Truax, 1999). It is perhaps unsurprising therefore that acousmatic approaches to sound have been embraced by researchers across a number of fields with an interest in human beings and societies.

A key early work bringing sonic approaches to the field of anthropology is Steve Feld's (1982: 97–8) ethnography of the Kaluli people, in which he introduces the concept of "acoustic epistemology," a particular kind of knowing born out of the body's experience of sound. Feld found that the Kaluli people of Papua New Guinea, over many generations, became highly adept at interpreting the rainforest environment and its myriad sonic moods. This enabled them to develop an "acoustemology" of the forest, or way of knowing that was inherently entangled with sounding and the experience of sound in a particular environment. Alongside the written publication of his findings, Feld released recordings of the Kaluli forest which were central to the dissemination of his findings and, in some cases, superseded the value of the written text. As he put it, "[W]hen you hear the way birds overlap in the forest . . . all of a sudden you can grasp something at a sensuous level that is considerably more abstract and difficult to convey in a written ethnography" (Feld and Brenneis, 2004: 465).

The influence of the work of Feld and others was such that, by the early 21st century, sound had found its way into a number of disciplines exploring more sensory approaches to research. As Feld and Brenneis (2004: 461) put it:

> Sound has come to have a particular resonance in many disciplines in the past decade. Social theorists, historians, literary researchers, folklorists and scholars in science and technology studies, and visual, performative and cultural studies, provide a range of substantively rich accounts.

And yet, music composition – specifically, notated instrumental composition – has remained conspicuously absent from most interdisciplinary work, with little impact outside specialised music circles. This complex relationship between interdisciplinary approaches to practice-as-research and notated instrumental composition is, in part, explained by an ongoing tendency to view the music score as a text.

Since the 19th century, the music score has "received textural status in a way that other, more kinetic, forms of practice have not" (Leedham and Scheuregger, 2020: 69). This has led to the assumption that a music score can function as the textual element of research on its own, without need for broader methodologies which contextualise and assess it. As the UK Council for Graduate Education observed in 2001, "[e]xperience from music suggests that it is possible for students and examiners who share a strong disciplinary language of practice to have a dialogue with little recourse to text" (quoted in Leedham and Scheuregger, 2020: 69). Since a score can only function as a text to those who have amassed the highly specialised skills required to read it as such, score-based music research continues to have relatively little broader impact, blunting the potential of music composition in interdisciplinary contexts.

Noting the highly specialised skills required to both write and analyse notated instrumental music does not classify the creation or reception of acousmatic musics as unskilled processes by contrast. As Rennie (2016: 18) points out, "[T]he act of field recording may be considered to contain fundamental compositional decision-making at its core." And yet, composing and analysing notated instrumental music remains an extremely specialised pursuit possible only after decades of intense and, generally, expensive training, often in a music department or conservatoire. By contrast, certain kinds of acousmatic approaches to sound are *relatively* more accessible to scholars who have been trained in fields such as anthropology, sociology or ethnomusicology, who may lack access to music composition training.

The focus of my work is notated instrumental music, and a key aim of this book is to develop methodologies which allow for the assessment and dissemination of practice-based research through embodied, performative means. The processes by which I work towards these ends will be discussed in more detail in Chapter 2. If we want music research to have greater impact across the arts, humanities and social sciences – and to catch up with other disciplines when it comes to debating and advancing the cause of practice-as-research – then it is essential to establish methodologies which allow this form to be considered in new ways. The continuing urgency of such a project is underlined by the fact that, as Leedham and Scheuregger (2020: 86) point out, the call to "devise our own [methodological] models" (Reeves, 2016: 57) set out by Reeves in response to Croft's provocation that composition is not really research, has remained largely unheeded. In order to consider *how* my project will contribute to this aim, it is necessary to explore the intertwining of evocative life-writing and music composition in my work, and it is these ways of knowing that will form the basis of the next chapter.

Notes

1 Here, Bolt refers not just to research in the so-called "hard sciences" but to all forms of qualitative and quantitative research which are not arts-/practice-based.
2 www.youtube.com/watch?v=R6D_3sBN3FM (Last accessed, 14th August 2019).
3 Since the witnessing and naming of lived experiences is central to the emancipatory politics of subaltern groups, and since the complexity and power of such experiences are best evoked through embodied accounts, there is a powerful intertwining of radical politics on the one hand and embodied methods on the other. Further works to consider in this vein include *Dust Tracks on the*

Road (1942/2017) by Zora Neale Hurston and *Drawn in Colour: African Contrasts (1960)* by Noni Jabavu, as well as work by Audre Lorde (2017), Bulkin et al. (1984) and Gloria Anzaldúa (2012) alongside collected volumes edited by Moraga and Anzaldúa (1981) and Grewal (1988).

4 See Stévance and Lacasse (2017) and Doğantan-Dack (2015).

2 Ways of Knowing

The entanglement of evocative life-writing and music composition is central to this project and – I could add – to my life. Over the past few years, I have become increasingly attuned to the reciprocal and iterative relationship between life experience and music composition in my own practice. This is not merely to say that the music I write is affected by the things I experience – this is unsurprising. Instead, I refer to something more fundamental. For many years, I found that my music often grappled with concepts, ideas and sources of pain that reflected the events of my life in complex ways. This process was sometimes subconscious and invisible from the surface, such that it was only through many hours of deep analysis and reflection that connections could be drawn. In some cases, it seemed as if I turned to music to work things out, deferring to a world of sound in which moving amongst materials unlocked a way of knowing that remained out of reach when considering through other means. In any case, it became clear to me that there was something very interesting going on in the process of my composing. For me, music was not just an escape or an expression of life experience; it was an epistemology for understanding the world in new ways with the potential to *create* knowledge, challenge theories and change perceptions. This insight made me wonder how much of the detail of life remains elusive when we consider phenomena from a purely detached, constative perspective. How much do we miss when we bracket out a process as rich and complex as music composition from broader scholarly thought?

In order to explore such ways of knowing in this chapter, I will first consider the history of evocative life-writing, exploring how this method allows for certain insights about the self that pertain particularly to my project. Following this, I will explore the method of music composition, considering how its mutual tendency towards performativity means it combines well with evocative life-writing. Here, I will outline how enjoining these methods can contribute to the development of practice-based methods in music through rendering

DOI: 10.4324/9781003351450-2

tangible the multi-faceted (and sometimes, mysterious) nature of arts practice. Next, I will consider instances when both evocative life-writing and music composition have been employed in studies of diaspora, sketching out where my particular project can add to these fields. Finally, I will outline the methods employed in my work, describing an approach based on a triangular circuit which continually moves back and forth between theory, practice and experiential knowledge.

Evocative Life-Writing

Evocative life-writing, which came to particular prominence in the academy around the 1990s (see e.g. Ellis, 1993, 1995, Ellis and Bochner, 1996; Reed-Danahay, 1997; Ronai, 1995), is a method of qualitative research in which the author's narrative self-reflection plays a central role. It is often characterised as a synthesis of postmodern autobiography and postmodern ethnography (Reed-Danahay, 1997: 1)[1] and developed at least in part due to the reflexive turn in anthropology (Clifford and Marcus, 1986)[2] and other disciplines (Clifford, 1986: 14). It deals with the detailed minutiae of life (Abu-Lughod, 1991: 150; Willis and Trondman, 2000: 11–12) and "[shares] the storytelling feature with other genres of self-narrative but [transcends] mere narration of self to engage in cultural analysis and interpretation" (Chang, 2008: 43). Various forms of writing have the potential to be considered examples of evocative life-writing, including life histories, native ethnographies, confessional tales and reflexive ethnographies, but central to this status is their capacity to "combine cultural analysis and interpretation with narrative details" (Chang, 2008: 46). That is to say, a personal story that is not reflected on, analysed or considered in a broader social context – for example, certain kinds of autobiography or memoir – would not be considered an example of evocative life-writing.

A central tenet of evocative life-writing is the notion that the self is produced through experience in the social world at the same time as the social world is produced through and by experiences of the self (Bakan, 2016: 9; Chang, 2008; Jones et al., 2013). Consequently, personal story is utilised not merely to address anecdotal experience but, rather, to speak to much broader concerns and connect "the personal story . . . to [the] universality" (Bakan, 2016: 9). This constant slippage between very specific personal experience and broader questions of cultural analysis and interpretation is evidenced in the work of Motzafi-Haller (1997), whose account focuses on her life experience in order to explore the personal and political motivations for research. Her writing encompasses her early childhood experiences in Israel, her research in Botswana, her establishment of an academic "home" in North America and eventual return to Israel to study the Mizrahim communities as a "native researcher." In so doing, she explores "the researcher's positioning in society and history and the kind of research agenda and understanding such personal background shapes" (Motzafi-Haller, 1997: 216–17). She therefore makes use of evocative life-writing to connect personal experience to broader, structural concerns against the backdrop of what it means to be differentially Othered (and not) in various social and professional contexts.

Similarly, my own project continuously slips between intensely personal reflections and broader cultural concerns. I consider on the one hand my feelings of internalised Otherness as a result of my experiences across British and Iranian identities, at the same time exploring broader questions of double-consciousness (Du Bois, 1994; Martinez, 2002; Gilroy, 1993; Anzaldúa, 2012) and diaspora (Clifford and Dhareshwar, 1989; Clifford, 1994, 1997; Gilroy, 1991, 1993; Brah and Coombes, 2000; Kalra et al., 2005). While such topics have been discussed at great length in academic literature, evocative life-writing has the potential to enrich such terms with embodied and personal detail.

Another key aspect of evocative life-writing is its rejection of positivist notions of truth and fiction. Here, writing is not an attempt to understand the reality of "what happened" since it views such an ideal as fundamentally false. It recognises that narrative accounts of lived experience are always a version, translation, or construction of events through the prism of both the past and the present. As Leggo puts it, narrative is always "a hermeneutic search, an ongoing process of presenting and representing, of change and exchange, of selection and election" (Leggo, 2005: 122), and evocative life-writing foregrounds this process rather than shying away from it. As a result, evocative life-writing has a tendency to consider experiences that are often left out of scholarly research because of the ways they resist positivist analysis. These include the struggle to find an academic job (Herrmann, 2012), the death of a lover with a terminal illness (Ellis, 1995), inter-racial dating in a rural American town (Ellis, 2009) and the loss of a mother to dementia (Bakan, 2016). A powerful example of such work is Carol Rambo Ronai's account of child abuse by her parents (Ronai, 1995). She offers searing details of this lived experience and yet makes no claims to "truth," instead presenting a "layered account . . . an impressionistic sketch" which offers readers layers of experience and encourages them to construct their own interpretation of the writer's narrative (Ronai, 1995: 396). This not only foregrounds the necessary constructedness of the account but also brings the reader deeper into the text such that it is they who "reconstruct the subject, thus projecting more of themselves into it, and taking more away from it" (Ronai, 1995: 396).

Similarly, in relation to my own story, I do not aim to capture the past with accuracy but, rather, to engage with my own self-narrative as a *material* to be followed and explored. Here, there is a particular link to music composition – to be considered in more detail later – which also resists positivist analysis and shares with evocative life-writing a capacity to evoke ambiguity (Bartleet and Ellis, 2009: 13). Thus, evocative life-writing uses writing not merely to reflect or report on reality but, rather, as a means of physically handling narratives of the past in order to explore constructions of the self and broader culture. As Leggo puts it, "[A]utobiographical writing is not capturing the past. . . . [It] is about re-creating a sense of self, re-visiting the past in order to render renewed versions of experience" (Leggo, 2005: 122).

Another key aspect of evocative life-writing is its unique capacity to highlight and embrace vulnerability and uncertainty in order to promote personal growth (Jones et al., 2013; Ellis and Bochner, 2006). In such forms of writing, disclosure with purpose is utilised not only to bring insight to our critical-analytical understanding of terms and concepts but also for its therapeutic potential for both author and reader alike. Consequently, evocative life-writing can be seen as:

> a method for figuring out life and writing through difficult experiences . . . [with] explicit and intentional directedness toward others, either through the offering of insight that might help those who relate to a person's experience or in a desire for others to bear witness to particular struggles.
>
> (Jones et al., 2013: 35)

Here, we can see that evocative life-writing tends strongly towards the pole of performativity within Bolt's model. This is because it self-consciously prioritises direct material engagement over detached observation and aims to affect the world rather than to describe or report on it, encouraging readers "to care, to feel, to empathize, and to do something, ultimately, 'to act'" (Ellis and Bochner, 2006: 433). It also explicitly engages with aspects of human life often considered unscholarly, such as experience, emotion and pain, and the expressly performative methods of evocative life-writing have the capacity to shed new light on such embodied experiences. Through these means, evocative life-writing centres the causes and effects of the researcher's own intervention in their work, eschewing solely detached and transcendent observation in a process which involves getting your hands dirty.

Jess Moriarty's (2013) *Leaving the Blood In: Experiences with an Autoethnographic Doctoral Thesis* is a powerful example of the performativity of evocative-life writing which can help illustrate some of these discussions. It uses her experiences as a PhD researcher to explore the dynamics and demands of research in the context of an increasingly neoliberal university environment. Her account contrasts first-person testimony (theoretically contextualised) with poetry and dramatic "scenes," offering, in her own words, "a highly charged, creatively written text that explicitly links autobiographical experiences with the social/cultural group under study without claiming objectivity" (Moriarty, 2013: 70). She engages in personal introspection and emotional disclosure in a way that highlights broader structural questions of power within academia. The format of an ethnodrama is effectively used for this purpose, particularly in a scene depicting a tense interaction between Moriarty and a senior colleague at university:

IMPACT – SCENE 2

Office at the university. JESS sits at her desk with her back to the door, typing furiously. Her e-mail pings and she stops work to look at whatever has arrived in her inbox.

JESS: (laughs) Oh that's a good one!

JAN enters the office. JAN is also in her 30s and head of the school that JESS is in; she grimaces as she sees JESS laughing and not working.

JAN: Something funny?
JESS: *(turning round)* Oh, hello Jan, I didn't hear you knock?
JAN: I didn't. We run an open door policy.
JESS: Of course.
    . . .
    Uncomfortable silence.
JAN: There is one thing; a lot of your work doesn't have anything in the title that can directly tie you to the school.
JESS: It's mainly about creativity and personal development.
JAN: That's what I mean. It isn't always relevant is it?
JESS: Oh?
JAN: I just wanted to ask you if you could put the word 'Literature' in some of your titles.
JESS: I could . . .
JAN: . . . after all, you don't want it all to be meaningless when it comes to the REF?
JESS: Meaningless?

(Moriarty, 2013: 70–1)

The tone of such an exchange reflects the increasing gulf between the ideals of research and the everyday machinations of the university as a business. Moreover, it stands in stark contrast to Moriarty's feelings about the imminent birth of her first child, evocatively expressed some pages later in the form of a poem.

> We have imagined
> bathing you in a bucket,
> deciding whose nose you ended up with,
> blaming each other for your stubborn streak.
>
> When you arrive
> it will be like everything and nothing
> we've been dreaming of.
> You're already better than our every wish.
>
> (Moriarty, 2013: 72–3)

Contrasting the pressures of the REF[3] on the one hand with the joy and excitement of new parenthood on the other elucidates the ways in which contemporary academic life overlooks the personal narratives that lie behind research outputs. This causes us to reflect on the structure of contemporary academia and the extent to which it exists in tension with a fulfilling home life. In this way, Moriarty's work makes effective use of ethnodrama to show us the character of Jess from multiple angles, at times presenting Moriarty as the "I" of the work, at others turning her into a character to be observed, presenting the "overlaps, stops and starts . . . the splintered narratives of my real life" (Moriarty, 2013: 62).

The Evocative Autoethnographic I: The Relational Ethics of Writing About Oneself (2013) by Lydia Turner is another important example of evocative life-writing. Turner makes use of multiple constructed characters as a means of questioning and destabilising her account. In one section, she writes a letter to her father expressing the pain of her childhood, telling him, "I know you did the best you could do with us Dad, but unfortunately it fell short" (Turner, 2013: 219). This revelation is immediately followed by a reply from her father (which we later learn was written by Turner herself), in which the veracity of such a characterisation is questioned:

> Reading what you wrote then, today, leaves me feeling sad. Do you really have to be so bitter about your childhood? Weren't your parents doing the best they could for you and can't you forgive them for their mistakes?
>
> (Turner, 2013: 219)

This shifting tone attunes us to the constructed nature of Turner's account while also undermining the primacy of her own voice within the text.

In a later section, Turner employs the authoritative "I" of academic writing to consider the ethics of evocative life-writing. Here she makes a clear argument that justifies the excavation of her life in a way that will necessarily include the lives of others:

> If I were to write about *my* reflections on others' words to or about me, asking permission from the originators of these words might be a moot point. I would argue that my experience is my construction of events. Within a constructed ontology, there ceases to be "factual" accounts which can be identified as the 'true' version of events, there are just different constructions of an event, or moment in history.
>
> (Turner, 2013: 220)

This analysis is immediately followed by a text from an unknown character who we glean is in a relationship with "Sarah," a practitioner of evocative life-writing who feels abandoned and shut out by her practice.

> What's with all this fucking auto stuff? Being authentic while being ethical. . . . She tells me that we "should" be thinking about the effect we have on others around us, but then appears to be blissfully unaware of how her behaviour affects others, how it affects me. . . . I don't crop up in her work, anywhere! I find out what she is up to by reading her latest draft. . . . The "participants" who share your life aren't mentioned. What about their ethical rights???
>
> (Turner, 2013: 220)

Such a shifting text – contrasting different voices and modes of writing – unveils the potential gulf between the "I" of research and the self of personal relationships: how the public positions we take on matters of research ethics may belie the complex relationships in turmoil as a result of these same decisions; how positions we present as faits accomplis due to the normalisation of the objective, authoritative account in academic writing may actually be the subject of a great deal more struggle; how we are all, at one time or another, hypocritical, wrong, bitter or unfair and that these qualities – which are flattened out by dominant discourses of writing – may bear on the research we produce.

Drawing on this work and others, I explore the performative nature of evocative life-writing through the use of non-standard textual formats which encourage an embodied relationship to the words on the page. A key example of this approach can be found in Chapter 3, where I use a number of conflicting, cross-cutting narratives to dramatically represent my experiences of diaspora and the concomitant state of double-consciousness. This chapter juxtaposes a discussion of theories of diaspora and double-consciousness on the one hand with vignettes, memories and "scenes" exploring my experience of such terms on the other. This section shifts abruptly between such narratives, overlapping texts in ways that disrupt the flow and force the reader to move backwards and forwards while reading. Crucially, the splitting of these texts attempts to represent the experience of fragmentation as a result of double-consciousness, pulling the reader into a rough approximation of this state. This structure also draws attention to the ways in which scholarly and personal narratives intertwine, at times connecting and following each other, at others diverging or opening up new and distinct paths. It is in the complex relationship *between* texts that the role of the reader comes to the fore, encouraging them to make links between what might seem to be disconnected narratives and uncover the meanings that exist amongst the various parts being presented.

A second example of performative work with text in this book can be found in Chapter 4: specifically, the analysis of *I Am the Spring, You Are the Earth* (one of the two compositions that form the basis of this book). The wandering quality of sound in this piece becomes a means for thinking through Ingold's (2008) notion of travel as "wayfaring," a concept that will be explored more later in relation to theories of diaspora. Drawing on a notion of *ductus* as "the way by which a work leads someone through itself" (Carruthers, 2013: 190) ,the formatting of this chapter encourages the reader/listener to experience both the music of *I Am the Spring, You Are the Earth* and the text-based discussion of it as an unfolding journey which echoes the flow-like nature of wayfaring. In this way, the text gestures towards a kind of movement defined by ebb and flow, unveiling insight gradually as the reader traverses the narrative. In contrast to the fragmented texts of Chapter 3 which imply the splittings of double-consciousness, the undulating, unfolding and open-ended quality of the text which describes and explores *I Am the Spring, You Are the Earth* gestures towards a kind of dynamism that could point towards a reconciliation of double-consciousness as a form of psychic splitting.

Music Composition

Of course, the aim of this book is to combine the methods of evocative life-writing with music composition, and it is to this latter approach to which I now turn. An essential similarity between evocative life-writing and music composition is the way both approaches resist constative contemplation, instead embracing complexity, ambiguity and embodied knowledge. This is because they are both essentially performative methods which involve forms of practical engagement with materials

(Bolt, 2016: 137). As has been discussed previously, Tim Ingold's notion of "making" outlines how the vibrancy of materials bears on the relationship with the artisan in practices of making:

> The maker [is] . . . a participant in amongst a world of active materials. These materials are what he has to work with, and in the process of making he "joins forces" with them.
>
> (Ingold, 2013: 21)

These qualities are also observed in discussions of music practice as a specific kind of 'making'. As Bresler writes:

> Music is produced by physical movement – the voice or an instrument which functions as the extension of the body, where the performer unites with the instrument to produce sound. . . . [I]n performance . . . music is experienced, not as something given to the body, but as something done through and with the body.
>
> (2005: 176–7)

While popular images abound of the detached composer genius who designs the whole form of a work in their mind and then simply follows this blueprint to bring the piece to life in the material world, such a (constative) model runs counter to the practicalities of artistic research. As has been noted, composers follow the forces and flow of their sonic materials through processes of doing and handling to bring the work into being in direct correspondence with the vitality of these materials. This loop is a recursive one such that *both* maker and materials are concomitantly produced through ongoing performative relationships of handling.

Indeed, reflecting on my own practice as a composer causes me to consider the ways in which my ongoing work with sound has produced a sense of knowing that is expressed through my body. Over decades of working with this material, I have developed a kind of intuition that guides me through the millions of creative decisions that outline the shape of an artwork. I consider this a way of knowing through which I understand *where* that material will flow in particular circumstances. Sometimes it takes the form of feeling magnetically pulled towards an idea when I compose or else an immediate understanding that something is *not quite right*. This feeling is guided by memories of past instances of music-making and the impact of countless life experiences and social forces on the way I approach sound.

We might be able to think of composing, therefore, as a version of what dance theorist Sheets-Johnstone refers to as *thinking in moving*:

> I am wondering the world directly, in movement; I am actively exploring its possibilities and what I perceive in the course of that wondering or exploration is enfolded in the very process of moving.
>
> (Sheets-Johnstone, 1981: 402)

Sheets-Johnstone (1981: 400) builds this concept in contrast to assumptions which both tie thinking and rationality together and construct "thought" as that which precedes and directs movement. Instead, she posits that *thinking in moving* interlaces thought and gesture such that bodily movement becomes a *means* for exploring and understanding the world. Bodily movement does not follow from thought or encapsulate thought; rather, it is its own kind of understanding through which the world is both perceived and created. Bringing this idea to bear on music composition might enable us to think about how composing is not a detached cognitive process which precedes and directs engagement with sound; rather, it is a knowing that is entangled in physical engagement with sound and the sounding environment. Through these means, the composer and their materials jointly explore a range of possibilities by means of processes of moving and handling. Since the flow of materials plays a key role in guiding the maker's movements, this allows for the fact that materials have an active role to play in producing the particular knowing that is inherent to the act of composing.

Certain aspects of evocative life-writing function in a very similar way. As described earlier, the material of evocative work is analytically contextualised storytelling which prioritises emotional power over descriptive accuracy and specificity over generalisation. Stories are not inert objects awaiting intervention by a human subject but are inherently "open-ended, inconclusive, and ambiguous" (Denzin, 2014: 6) materials which might "wander, twist and turn, changing direction unexpectedly" (Short et al., 2013: 2). Writing is thus not merely a method of documenting or inscribing a story; it is a means of correspondence which allows the writer to follow the flow of the story as a material in order to *write through it* (Jones et al., 2013: 35; Bakan, 2016: 9). Further, a story's narrative does not appear to the writer fully formed, but must be teased out through a process of handling, of turning the story over through reflection and reflexivity. This is an intensely material process which cannot be carried out at a safe, contemplative distance (Bartleet and Ellis, 2009: 10) and through which the writer is concomitantly produced. It forces the practitioner to wade into painful areas of their life to excavate narratives they may have hidden even from themself for years. It is more than mere analogy to say that to do evocative life-writing, you need a thick skin (Short et al., 2013: 10).

Entangling the methods of evocative life-writing on the one hand with music composition on the other, has the potential to progress the cause of music composition as a form of practice-based research with inter-disciplinary relevance. This is because this combined methodology allows us to speak in detail about the embodied ways of knowing that are central to composition as a particular, and largely remote, form of arts research that go untheorised when we use only constative, analytical research methods.

Untangling the details of music composition as a way of knowing involves translating into non-specialist language a process that is not necessarily amenable to this means of representation. But putting this practice into words *is* important, especially if my own aim is to use music composition as a means of reflecting on an extra-musical concept and, more broadly, to advance the cause of this method. Here, evocative life-writing acts as the crucial bridge between composing and language, filling in the narrative gap which can remain when trying to render into words the embodied ways of knowing that are central to music composition. This has the important effect of making composition as a bodily way of knowing more tangible to those who stand outside this specialism. Indeed, by intertwining music composition with evocative life-writing, perhaps we can finally work towards developing a vernacular for composing as an epistemology of interdisciplinary relevance.

Given this great potential in combining evocative life-writing with music composition, it is perhaps unsurprising that evocative life-writing is a method of growing popularity in music studies. Following the publication of Bartleet and Ellis' (2009) *Music Autoethnographies: Making Autoethnography Sing/Making Music Personal*, important conferences such as Beyond "Mesearch": Autoethnography, Self-Reflexivity, and Personal Experience as Academic Research in Music Studies (16–17 April 2018) convened by the Institute of Musical Research at University of London and The Autoethnography of Composition and the Composition of Autoethnography (17–18 June 2020) at University of Glasgow have shown the depth of this interest. See also a forthcoming 35-chapter volume entitled *The Routledge Companion to Autoethnography and Self- Reflexivity in Music Studies* edited by Christopher Wiley and Peter Gouzouasis, as well as work by Bakan (2016), Findlay-Walsh (2018), Gouzouasis and Ihnatovych (2016), Wiley (2019) and Hollingworth (2019).

Studies of Diaspora Through Evocative Life-Writing . . .

Against this backdrop of a combined methodology of evocative life-writing and music composition, it is now pertinent to consider how these two approaches will enable consideration of the concept of diaspora – a key concern of my work. Diaspora has been widely studied across the humanities and social sciences since the 1990s (see e.g. Clifford and Dhareshwar, 1989; Gilroy, 1991, 1993; Brah and Coombes, 2000; Kalra et al., 2005; Safran, 1991; Hall, 1990; Clifford, 1993, 1994; Tölölyan, 1991). Since this time, a small number of writers working in the field of diaspora studies have engaged forms of writing similar to evocative life-writing as a key methodology. Avtar Brah (1996: 6) uses what she terms "technologies of autobiographies" in the introduction of her *Cartographies of Diaspora* in order to highlight the "contradictions embodied in the production of identity." This technique is developed further in *Scent of Memory* (1999), where she interweaves discussion of an autobiography by Tim Lott (dealing with his mother's life and ultimate suicide in Southall, London) with Brah's own PhD research on the racism faced by South Asian families in this area. Amongst these two accounts, Brah's own voice emerges, addressing the tension that exists between different stories of the same area and drawing a picture of the complexity of "diaspora space" in London.

Alisse Waterston (2005) intertwines anthropological enquiry with evocative life-writing to narrate a story of the Jewish diaspora. Through recounting the biography of her father, an East European Jew displaced from Poland to Cuba and then Puerto Rico, she explores broad socio-historical currents – 20th-century nation building, genocide, the manufacturing of difference – from the point of view of the individual. Through such means, she interrogates the ways in which experiences of displacement and dictatorship imbricate with family dynamics, producing complex webs of anxiety and loss. As she puts it, "[My father's] sorrows become my sorrows, his losses my motivation to understand them" (Waterston, 2005: 53). Through processes of reflection she unravels the complexity of these diasporic lineages. This enables an exploration of the ways that troubling experiences are passed down through generations and how diaspora can be experienced as the ongoing "[search for] a place to be and to belong" (Waterston, 2005: 54), even when the desire for a lost homeland has long faded.

Kimberley J. Lau's *This Text Which Is Not One: Dialectics of Self and Culture in Experimental Autoethnography* (2002) evocatively explores the author's complex relationship to her Chinese-Japanese-American-Hawai'ian identity. In this work, she splits each page into three sections (left, top right and bottom right) to present a series of separate but concurrent narratives, each written in a different style and represented by a different font. The unconventional structuring of the narrative is more than just a matter of layout, and it brings its own insight to the topic of Lau's complex relationship to her identity.

There is no clear order in which to read Lau's text as a result of left-right reading conventions, and thus, the reader is left to make a decision about how to navigate their way through it. Moreover, the reader necessarily moves backwards and forwards through the text in order to finish sentences which run over a page, and thus, the linear movement of the work is disrupted. As such, the text is experienced less as a teleological march towards a conclusion, and more as a disrupted narrative which gains meaning through the ways that material is overlapped. Revelation appears gradually as you work your way through the article, and it is only when you are some pages in that it is revealed the work combines personal (left), theoretical (top right) and analytical narratives (bottom right) on the broader topic of identity, race and "emotional desire for an integrated, whole self" (Lau, 2002: 255).

Crucially, the "Lau" who is produced in this text is multivocal and fluid. We gradually learn that there is a gulf between Lau's practice as a scholar – which works to deconstruct notions of integrated identity – and her contrasting desire as an individual to seek and establish an authentic, whole self (Lau, 2002: 255). Both the unconventional layout and the genre of evocative life-writing are key to bringing this insight to light, enabling the theorisation of the important gap that exists between personal and scholarly positions.

My project builds on the ground established by some of the work discussed here but crucially intertwines an evocative account of my life experience of diaspora with my practice as a music composer. Interestingly, the relationship between music composition and studies of diaspora is much less well established despite a variety of work in music studies exploring this term.

. . . And Music

The connections between diaspora studies and music are many and various, covering a variety of topics within the broader umbrella of music studies. The concept of diaspora has been considered a great deal from the vantage point of "academic" music scholarship, particularly across the sub-disciplines of sociology of music and ethnomusicology. This work takes a variety of forms and includes analysis of cultural artefacts born of diasporic and hybrid encounters (Hutnyk, 1998; Sharma, 1996); ethnographic investigation of music made in the diaspora (Ramnarine, 2007), analysis of discourses in music of the Black diaspora (Gilroy, 2001) and accounts of cosmopolitanism and migration and their effects on music (Gidal, 2010; Stokes, 1994). In general, these works tend towards the constative pole of methods, describing, analysing and critiquing this topic rather than engaging with it in a physical or embodied way.

Within this area, there is a significant amount of scholarship which explores the politics of diaspora from the point of view of particular music composers. It is important to note that this scholarship does not fall within the broad definition of "music composition" since no new music is being produced. Instead these are academic works within the sub-disciplines of music/musicology/ethnomusicology/sociology of music which use the life experiences of particular composers as a focal point for talking more broadly about the dynamics of diaspora. Many such works depict stories of individual musical development set against the backdrop of movement between the global south and colonial centre. A common biography involves a musician born in the global south who spends time in Europe or the US to establish their careers in western classical music, bringing with them knowledge and experience of their local musical traditions. These ideas are integrated into their broader practice in western classical music with the potential to produce new hybrid forms. This process highlights colonial balances of power and points to experiences of identity and Othering as they relate to music.

For example, the life story of Nigerian composer Samuel Akpabot (1932–2000) follows a familiar path of diasporic movement in which musicians seek training and opportunities that might not be available in the global south. Born in Nigeria, Akpabot moved to London at the age of 21 to study at the Royal College of Music. After returning home to work at the Nigerian Broadcasting Corporation, he relocated to the US in the 1960s to further his studies in composition and ethnomusicology, eventually receiving his doctorate from Michigan State University (Sadoh, 2010). Perhaps unsurprisingly, Akpabot's music reflects these diasporic movements, drawing at once from Yoruba, Igbo, Efik and Ibibio cultures, as well as from western classical music and African American music traditions (Sadoh, 2010: 79). That Akpabot's story of travel is reflected in his music facilitates a discussion of hybridity and fusion as a result of colonial imbalances of power through attendance to his art.

Tōru Takemitsu is another composer whose musical style is intertwined with experiences of travel and diaspora. He described himself as a Japanese composer of western classical music who, although frequently travelling to the west, could never compose while outside Japan (Hung Lie, 2012: 281, footnote 9). He avoided traditional Japanese music in his youth and even "denied" his Japaneseness as a result of traumatic experiences during World War II (Takemitsu, 2010: 53). It was not until the 1960s (when he was in his 30s) that he first began to incorporate ideas from Japanese music into his work, composing, among other important works, *An Autumn Ode* (1962) for Sho and Orchestra, and *November Steps* (1967) for Biwa, Shakuhachi and Orchestra. Here, Takemitsu's life story becomes a means through which to consider narratives of self-Othering and the psychic effects of colonial narratives.

As Omojola (2007) has shown, the music of Nigerian composer Fela Sowande (1905–1987) is another instance in which narratives of diaspora, travel and music intertwine. As a result of his history of travel and displacement, Sowande's music draws on various sources, including European classical styles, Yoruba songs and negro spirituals. Sowande's affiliation with the pan-African movement was reflected in his affiliation with Black music, providing "a creative forum for demonstrating the kinship between African and African-American cultures." At the same time, Sowande's success relied heavily on the colonial state (receiving many commissions and performances via the BBC), and he struggled to find fame in his native Nigeria, at least in part due to the political instability caused by the aftermath of colonial rule (Omojola, 2007: 165). Thus, Sowande's life and work become lenses through which to consider colonial dynamics, identity formation in music, pan-Africanism and the dynamics of hybridity and fusion.

As noted previously, none of the scholarship considered here falls into the category of music composition because no new music is produced through such work. Furthermore, the preceding work all tends towards the constative arm of research since it reproduces a model of detached observation, analysis and criticism. Turning to work which involves practice-based means (and focusing only on musicians working in the context of the Iranian diaspora) yields a great variety of work which tends more towards performativity. Some key pieces include *Soliloquy* (2001) by Sussan Deyhim and Shirin Neshat, *All of You* (2010) by Hooshyar Khayam and Amir Eslami, *Sympathy-24* (2016) by Anahita Abbasi, *It's Still Autumn* (2019) by Kayhan Kalhor and Rembrandt Frerichs Trio, *We, the Innumerable* (2020) by Niloufar Nourbakhsh and *Daste Ma* (2022) by Roxanna Albayati and Mahsa Salali. There is huge variety amongst such pieces: from works which explicitly focus on questions of diaspora, identity and belonging (e.g. Abbasi; Albayati and Salali) to those whose political themes (Nourbakhsh) or presence of solo female singers (Deyhim and Neshat) make them inherently diasporic creations (since they would be illegal to perform in Iran) and from those whose collaborative style is inherently reliant on diasporic encounters (e.g. Kalhor)[4] to work born of diasporic performer/composers who have studied both Iranian and western classical musics in Iran and abroad (e.g. Khayam and Eslami).

While these varied examples show that there are many instances in which music functions as a means for thinking about diaspora, there is a common lacuna in much of this work, itself partly a result of the ongoing gulf between practice-as-research in music composition and theorymaking. Works by Deyhim and Neshat; Kalhor; Nourbakhsh, Albayati and Salali; and Abassi noted earlier each offer unique and thoughtful expressions of diasporic experience, but the lack of written accompaniment to these pieces means they remain largely uncontextualised from a theoretical standpoint. Further, while Sadoh (2010), Hung Lie (2012) and Omojola (2007) all discuss musical works as the *output* of diasporic experience, they tend to bracket out the practice of music composition in this process. This results in an account that does little to explore the ways in which music composition as a practice can contribute to our theoretical understanding of diaspora. Indeed, as part of a broader lack of methodologies which allow for the communication of practice-derived knowledge in music (Leedham and Scheuregger, 2020: 66), there is a tendency to overlook music composition as a method for problematising theories of diaspora. As a result, music composition is considered largely as the output of diasporic encounters rather than as a process which could directly contribute to constructions of diaspora on a theoretical level.

Tripartite Model

Against this backdrop of work which engages variously with the methods of evocative life-writing and music composition in the context of studies of diaspora, my own account emerges with a very specific aim. To reiterate, I engage embodied approaches to music practice (grounded in enactivism) with the aim of adding unique nuance and detail to our understanding of diaspora. This will underline the performative nature of all knowledge-producing practices since physical engagement with the world is the *fundamental* basis of cognition and experience. Moreover, through deep engagement with my compositional work, this book aims to contribute to methodologies for practice-as-research in music. Specifically, it will explore how an intertwined use of evocative life-writing and music composition can enable deep exploration of extra-musical theoretical concepts. Finally, through a focus on acoustic instrumental music, this book aims to advance the practice-as-research credentials of this form, bringing it into discussions of broad relevance in the humanities and social sciences.

In order to work towards such aims, I have developed a tripartite model of methods which is depicted in the diagram in Figure 2.1. This shows a triangular circuit connecting the three points of analytical knowledge (theory), practice (composition) and experiential knowledge (evocative life-writing).

Analytical knowledge
(theory)

Practice ◄──────────► Experiential knowledge
(composition)   (evocative life-writing)

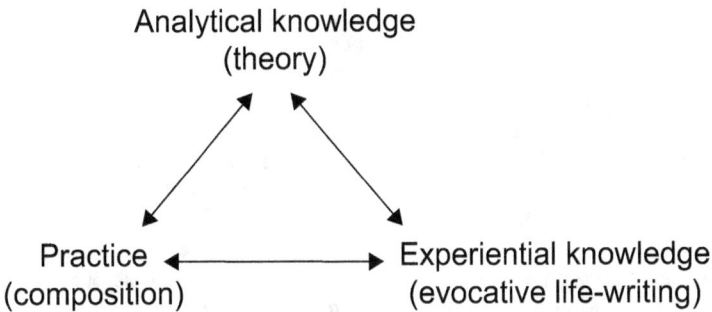

Figure 2.1 Triangulation of methods in this project

"Analytical knowledge" is a label for the theoretical work I explore throughout this book, including discussions of double-consciousness (Du Bois, 1994; Martinez, 2002; Anzaldúa, 2012), diaspora (Gilroy, 1993; Hall, 1990; Clifford, 1994), travel and place (Ingold, 2007, 2008) and making (Ingold, 2013). "Practice" relates to music composition, defined as processes of making and moving that engage with sound as a material. "Experiential knowledge" refers to my lifetime of experience of double-consciousness, diaspora and the process of music composition and is represented through a range of writing styles broadly defined as evocative life-writing.

As was explored extensively in Chapters 1 and 2, this intertwining of methods has a number of important outcomes which can be briefly summarised as:

1 Rendering tangible the complex, embodied processes of music composition so it can contribute to discussions of extra-musical theory.
2 Bringing discussion of notated instrumental music to greater relevance across the arts, humanities and social sciences.
3 Adding embodied, evocative detail to our concept of diaspora.
4 Underlining the embodied nature of all knowledge-producing practices.

In practice, this means that musical works, alongside personal narrative subsequently analysed, are used in this book as settings to consider the ways in which the concept of diaspora has left an indelible mark on my life. I scrutinise this term from the viewpoint of my own experience but specifically in order to add greater nuance to the broader theoretical conceptualisation of such a key concept.

For example, the lifelong impact of this term is manifested in the relationships I set in motion in my various compositions. Subsequent analysis of these works then brings to the surface aspects of personal experience that might otherwise have been inaccessible through text writing alone. In some cases, compositions are explicitly guided by evocative reflection, setting up particular musical relationships because of the ways they evoke a personal experience related to diaspora. In others, composition proceeds intuitively, and it is on reflection that routes are opened up which enable personal experience to be reconsidered or repositioned. The entanglement of evocative life-writing and composition is then reflected back onto theory, facilitating deeper analysis of core concepts. This process will play out in Chapter 4 where I consider in detail the concept of diaspora through in-depth analysis of my life experience alongside the pieces *Tradition-Hybrid-Survival* and *I Am the Spring, You Are the Earth*.

Notes

1 It is also important to note the lineage of writing by authors of colour and feminist authors which lay the groundwork for the development of evocative life-writing as a discipline. Some key examples of proto auto-ethnographic writing include Du Bois (1994), Fanon (2008), Cixous (1976), hooks (1991), Hurston (1942), Jabavu (1960), Lorde (2017), Bulkin et al. (1984) and Anzaldúa (2012).
2 There are, however, key differences between a work of reflexive ethnography and a piece of evocative life-writing. As Deck (1990: 246) outlines with reference to the work of Marjorie Shostak (1983) and Vincent Crapanzano (1980), these ground-breaking reflexive fieldwork accounts still employ a hierarchy of voices to validate material and marginalise autobiographical details from the core of the text (normally to an epilogue and/or prologue) and focus only on the reflexivity of the author as it pertains to their time in the field.
3 Research Excellence Framework, a UK government initiative begun in 2014, which required universities to report on the quality of their research output in order to secure continued public funding.
4 Practices of combining elements from both Iranian and western music date back to the early 20th century and are often referred to as *musiqi-ye talfighi*, or fusion music. For more information on the genre of *musiqi-ye talfighi*, see Lolavar (2021b: 63ff).

3   Double-Consciousness, Diaspora and Me

The terms "diaspora" and "double-consciousness" have been mentioned a great deal up to this point. Indeed, they are both, simultaneously, terms which play a central role in my project and concepts which have had a major impact on my life. At this juncture, I will consider both in detail, exploring their theoretical bases from a number of angles and reflecting on the ways in which they can potentially come together to form a therapeutic and personal healing. To work towards these aims, I will first outline the theory of double-consciousness as an internalised form of subject-object dualism through which the individual looks upon themself through the eyes of a dominant and hostile culture. My own experiences of this state were the starting point for this book, which explores ways out of such forms of dislocation. Next, diaspora is considered as a frame which offers a potential resolution of double-consciousness due to the way it moves beyond subject-object binaries. These key terms will be sketched out in this chapter and then analysed in detail through a three-part methodology enjoining theory, practice and experiential knowledge in chapter 4.

In order to highlight the embodied and performative nature of this project, discussions of double-consciousness and diaspora will be disrupted by other styles of text writing which explore my personal relationship to these terms. Drawing on the work of Lau (2002), Moriarty (2013) and Turner (2013), who all use a variety of text styles in their writing, I here create a fragmentary, multi-layered text that moves continuously between analytical and embodied forms of knowledge. These varied text styles include diary entries, experiential vignettes, screenplays (where both real and imagined experiences are written up as scenes from a play/film), email correspondence and real-life news clippings.[1] All these forms of writing were gathered during an intense period of reflection on my relationship to diaspora and double-consciousness, enabling me to consider how these varied experiences have impacted my life in ways that periodically align with/contradict more linear scholarly narratives. This disrupted style gestures towards my own experiences of these topics

DOI: 10.4324/9781003351450-3

and itself highlights some of the splittings of double-consciousness as I experience them. In these ways, this text attempts to discourage passive interaction since the reader has to constantly move backwards and forwards through the text, affecting a kind of correspondence through which meaning is ascertained. It also gestures towards a kind of embodiment of the fragmentation of double-consciousness as I experience it, encouraging the reader to understand this concept in a potentially new way.

Double-Consciousness

Du Bois's concept of double-consciousness (which most notably appears in the 1903 publication *The Souls of Black Folk*) describes the psychic experience of embodying two oppositional ideas – the "negro" and the "American" – within one human self. This experience exerts huge emotional pressure on the individual who is overwhelmed by:

> this sense of always looking at one's self through the eyes of others, of measuring one's soul by the tape of a world that looks on in amused contempt and pity. One ever feels his two-ness – an American, a Negro; two souls, two thoughts, two unreconciled strivings; two warring ideals in one dark body, whose dogged strength alone keeps it from being torn asunder.
>
> (Du Bois, 1994: 2)

Double-consciousness leaves the Black American unable to conceive of themself outside racist structures which devalue and degrade their humanity. This places the individual in a constant state of tension, essentially splitting their personhood into two warring parts (Martinez, 2002: 170).

As noted previously, Du Bois uses the metaphor of the veil to represent the divide between those who live in this state of double-consciousness and those who do not. In establishing this concept, he describes his childhood experience of a white girl refusing a card from him in such a way that he suddenly understood the racial divide between himself and his white classmates. As he puts it, "[T]hen it dawned upon me with a certain suddenness that I was different from the others . . . shut out from their world by a vast veil" (Du Bois, 1994: 2). The veil has been variously interpreted as representing:

> race itself and its impact on the lives of Black Americans, the racial lens through which White Americans view Black Americans, and the double-consciousness with which Black Americans experience their world.
>
> (Schaefer, 2008: 412)

The notion of the veil thus encompasses a variety of racialised experiences which include lived experience of racial discrimination, the perception and treatment of racialised

> My uncle Amin died today. Now my father and my uncle Taqi are the only boys left from the original family of ten.
>
> Uncle Ariya passed away at the age of 65 of a single, deadly heart attack. That being said, I'm sure several rounds of electric shock therapy – administered when he was in his 20s to cure him of his opium addiction – can't have helped. I didn't know about the treatment when I was a child and often wondered why he was so fragile. He seemed to exist behind a pane of glass.
>
> Amin officially died of a heart attack too, but part of me thinks it was retribution. He caused a lot of pain to a lot of people, including my parents. My father told me he cried when he heard the news and that he didn't expect he would. I sat with my dad and called my family in Iran to give my condolences. When he heard me speaking Farsi, he started to cry again.

communities by white groups *and* the ways in which racialised communities understand themselves and their experiences in the world.

While *The Souls of Black Folk* focuses largely on the experiences of Black communities in America and, indeed, draws a great deal from Du Bois's personal experiences – "[N]eed I add that I who speak here am bone of the bone and flesh of the flesh of them that live within the Veil?" (Du Bois, 1994: 1) – his work also allows for the broadening of double-consciousness to other colonial contexts. As Du Bois puts it, "The problem of the twentieth century is the problem of the color-line, – the relation of the darker to the lighter races of men in Asia and Africa, in America and the islands of the sea" (Du Bois, 1994: 10).

Du Bois's framing is crucial also to the work of Frantz Fanon, who explores a psychic experience similar to double-consciousness but expands the reach to include all racialised colonial subjects. In his 1952 work *Black Skin, White Masks*, Fanon draws deeply on his personal experiences to consider how the raced subject is *produced* by such relations of colonialism such that "the Negro has to wear the livery that the white man has sewed for him" (Fanon, 2008: 22). Thus, the subaltern Black/colonial subject is a creation of structures of white supremacy, embedding a relationship of inferiority which is essential to the

> INT. (Interior) Soosan's living room, evening
>
> SOOSAN and WILL sit on the sofa and watch television; on screen, a teacher talks to his class about race.

Voice-Over (ON SCREEN)
The teachers have all been trained to run affinity groups.

Male teacher, white, early 30s, earnest. Stands amongst a group of 11- and 12-year-olds sitting in a circle of chairs

Male teacher (ON SCREEN)
Okay, so outside please; can we have the people who associate them-selves as a white person, from a white ethnic background – you're going to go next door. In this room, people who associate themselves as Black or Middle Eastern or Asian. . . . You're going to remain in this room.

V.O. (ON SCREEN)
The idea is to create a space for different races to discuss their experi-ences without fear of judgement before coming back together to air issues and problems which wouldn't normally come out.

FARRAH, 12-year-old girl, white and South Asian background, long dark hair, slightly crooked teeth

Farrah (ON SCREEN)
Where do I go?

Farrah looks to the children on her left and right for guidance.

maintenance of colonial rule. As Fanon puts it, "[H]e [a Negro] lives in a society that makes his inferiority possible, in a society that derives its stability from the perpetuation of this complex" (Fanon, 2008: 74). The psychological effects of such an experience lead to a splitting of the self in line with double-consciousness as set out by Du Bois.

Fanon further shows how subaltern groups take on these racialised subjecthoods to such an extent that they jostle for power by positioning themselves on a colour line: a scale of race and culture which is inher-ently built on white supremacy:

> The Frenchman does not like the Jew, who does not like the Arab, who does not like the Negro. . . . The Arab is told: "If you are poor, it is because the Jew has bled you and taken everything from you." The Jew is told: "You are not of the same class as the Arab because you are really white and because you have Einstein and Bergson."
>
> (Fanon, 2008: 76–7)

Drawing on this notion of a scale of relative distance from whiteness and taking up the metaphor of the veil once more, we might consider how the material of the veil is differentially transparent or opaque for particu-lar subjects based on their claims to white

The first time I was ever referred to as a person of colour was in an in-terview for *I Care If You Listen* in 2017. The interview was conducted in that slightly annoying fashion of the interviewer sending their questions over email for me to write my own responses – so really the interview was written *me*, not the interviewer. But in any case, question three asked me if I had any "anecdotes or words of advice for women and people of color [sic] navigating the sexism and racism of the contemporary music scene," a question which implicitly assumed that I was both these things. I genuinely thought there had been some sort of mistake, that they had mixed me up with someone else. I read through the other questions to make sure that they were meant for me. I almost emailed the interviewer to explain that she had got me confused with someone else. In the end, I did my best to answer the question, referring generally to "minorities" in contemporary music without actually defining myself in relation to *that* word.

proximity and, further, how the presence or absence of particular groups (constructed as more or less white than others) can cause the shape of the veil to contort and change. To take Fanon's example, while the Jew may be assigned whiteness in relation to the Arab, in the absence of this latter subject (and their greater racialisation), the Jew reverts to their status as the Other to the Frenchman, who remains the ideal white subject. That is, while Du Bois's construction of double-consciousness focuses on the experiences of the Black (man) in white America, it might be expanded to incorporate a scale of experiences of Othering which depend on the differential closeness to whiteness assigned to those subjects by structures of white supremacy.

Iranian Double-Consciousness

I will now explore the extent to which the concept of double-consciousness can be usefully applied to Iranian identities through a consideration of the racialised Othering of Iranian bodies. Iranians are an ambiguously raced group with variegated and complex experiences of race and ethnicity. While some Iranians continue to make claims to whiteness, many experience a cultural browning as a result of histories of colonisation, media narratives of Iranian people and culture, travel restrictions and surveillance at airports. This Othering of Iranians means they are vulnerable to experiences of double-consciousness as raced bodies entangled in colonial discourses.

PUPIL 1, 12 year old boy, Black, glasses

Pupil 1 (ON SCREEN)
(Laughing) You can stand in between the doors.

PUPIL 2, 11 year old girl, East Asian, hair in a ponytail

Pupil 2 (ON SCREEN)

You can choose.

Farrah still looks unsure.

Farrah (ON SCREEN)

Where do I go? Do I stay in here, or do I go out there? I'm used to being around people who are like . . . white. I'm half white and half Asian, and I don't know which room to go in.

A short silence

Pupil 1 (ON SCREEN)

You're in our room, okay; you stay here with us; you belong here.

They all laugh and clap.

[19:38] Soosan: Baba, I have a question for you.
[19:39] Soosan: What race do you think you are?
[19:39] Soosan: If you had to write it on a form or whatever, what would you say?
[20:42] Dad: Iranian (from Arian) [sic].

It is a commonly held belief amongst Iranians that the etymological similarity between "Iranian" and "Aryan" signals the history of Iranians as a racially white people. As Maghbouleh (2017: 54–5) outlines, this belief stems largely from the Aryan myth constructed by Iranian politician Hassan Pirnia (1872–1935). In the shadow of traumatising loss of territory during the Qajar era (1789–1925), Pirnia claimed that the presence of the premodern term *ariya* (noble) in a Zoroastrian sacred text was a precursor to the racialised term "Aryan." Through mobilising the myth of Iranian peoples as Aryan and particularly contrasting this with Arabs labelled as Semitic, nationalist discourses tapped into the success of Aryan narratives in Europe to stress common roots between Iran and the culture of the "admired Europeans" (Motadel, 2014: 131). This myth was promoted as a national racial project in Iran under the two Pahlavi regimes (1925–1941, 1941–1979) such that it is common for Iranians who were born in this period – such as my father – to unproblematically claim their racial identity as

INT. SOOSAN is lying on the sofa in her living room, speaking to PARISA on the phone, afternoon

Soosan

Don't say that.

Parisa (Voice-Over)

Why not?

Soosan

Because I'm not, I don't identify as (pause) entirely white.

Parisa (V.O.)

But people think we're white all the time. . . . we are.

Soosan sits up, moves the phone to her left ear.

Soosan

I'm just not sure I like the idea that my ethnic identity is based on what other people think of me.

Parisa (V.O.)

Yeah but we've never been stopped and searched; we've never been called a racial slur.

Soosan

True, but that doesn't mean I define myself as totally white. And anyway, why should non-whiteness be defined entirely in terms of racism? There has to be some meaning to ethnic and racial identity that stands outside of oppression, otherwise we're basically letting racists define all the categories and their meaning.

Parisa (V.O.)

Yeah, but as a political category, it *is* about those things, and you and I have never been treated as anything other than white.

Soosan

That's not true. We get Othered.

white. The Aryan myth is steeped in Orientalism and white supremacy and is a clear attempt to move up the colour line identified by Fanon previously. Through mobilising the figure of Eurocentric racial science par excellence – the Aryan – "homegrown Orientalists" (Maghbouleh, 2017: 54) such as Pirnia attempt to load acclaim onto Iranian culture by aligning it with whiteness and separating it from that of their "racially inferior" Middle Eastern neighbours.

The self-Orientalising aspects of the Aryan myth emerge against the backdrop of Iran's colonial history. In 1907 the Anglo-Russian Entente divided Iran into three zones, one each for Britain and Russia and a third designated a "neutral zone" (Keddie, 2003: 69–70). The advent of WWI brought Iran – particularly the strategic importance of its location – to the attention of Ottoman and German forces, who invaded the country despite its expressed neutrality (Ansari, 2003: 22). The end of this conflict and the outbreak of the Russian revolution, accompanied by the discovery of oil in the "British" zone of the country in 1908 and subsequent establishment of the Anglo-Persian Oil Company (APOC), began a decades-long paternalistic relationship between Iran and Britain (Ansari, 2003: 30). Iranian sentiment

> I sit at my desk in London a little over 24 hours after President Trump ordered the assassination of General Qassem Suleimani – the leader of the Iranian Quds army – consumed by the familiar sense that my fragile British Iranian selfhood is about to shatter. Predictably, the news is covered in images of mass gatherings of Iranians – men beating their chests, women gripping their black chadors – an undertone of crazed savagery present throughout. I feel like I am being split in two.

> I struggle to disentangle my being from Orientalised representations of Middle Eastern barbarity to such an extent that the tone of such coverage causes me to fear and loathe myself. At the same time, I am aware of my positioning as an elite British voice: a voyeur from London observing from afar conflicts from which I am fundamentally safe and the beneficiary of systems of colonialism which amplify my voice more than any member of my extended family. As a British Iranian person, I am implicated as both object and subject within such systems of oppression, and the weight of this knowledge threatens the collapse of my internal self. I feel a deep fissure opening up inside me, a triggering of old wounds and a re-igniting of a sense of myself as broken, ambivalent and lost.

towards the British was largely hostile and suspicious. UK forces were popularly believed to have been involved in the 1921 coup which led to Reza Khan's eventual installment as Shah and establishment of the Pahlavi dynasty (Ansari, 2003: 27). British interests are similarly implicated in the 1941 abdication of Reza Shah and coronation of his son, Reza Pahlavi (Ansari, 2003: 83), as well as the 1953 coup toppling the popular nationalist Prime Minister Mohammad Mosaddegh (Ansari, 2003: 113). US forces were also implicated in this event and, after its success, became the de facto dominant power in Iran for much of the 20th century (Keddie, 2003: 132). With US backing, Reza Pahlavi continued the widespread programme of modernisation begun by his father, a central part of which involved the westernisation of many aspects of Iranian society and whose unpopularity fueled the Iranian revolution (Keddie, 2003: 135ff).

Paternalistic relationships between Iran, Britain and the US in the 20th century reproduce colonial narratives which, as Fanon has shown, racialise communities who live under ruling powers coded as white. In the contemporary context, Maghbouleh's (2017) research into Iranian American youth found that many experienced racialisation and racial discrimination throughout their lives. Representations of Iranian culture on television and in print media play a key role in reproducing biases about Iranian communities, offering a narrow range of narratives which contribute to a racialised Othering of these groups. A key discourse in this regard focuses on the plight of Iranian women, who (alongside women of the Middle East more generally) are constructed as oppressed, powerless and in need of salvation.

Calls for the so-called liberation of Middle Eastern women took on particular political significance in the era following the 9/11 attacks, such that contrasts between "liberated

1   Questions about your father:
    a   Does your dad support you being a musician?
    b   Do your mum and dad get on?
    c   What does your dad think about you having a boyfriend?
    d   Is your dad a Muslim?
    e   What does your dad think about you living the way you do?

2   Questions about Iran:
    a   Have you been to Iran?
    b   When you're there, do you cover up?
    c   What's it really like for women out there?

3   Comments about how you look:
    a   You don't look very Iranian.
    b   You look foreign.
    c   Where are you really from?

American women [and] oppressed Muslim/Arab/Middle Eastern women" were used to justify and explain the American invasions of Afghanistan (2001) and Iraq (2003) (Jabbra, 2006: 329). As Malek (2006: 361ff) has pointed out, memoirs written by Iranian or Iranian American women found particular success in the US publishing market in this period, forming part of a post-9/11 atmosphere in which American readers were curious for "real stories" emanating from a country firmly placed within the "Axis of Evil." In this context, writing by Iranian women was "confined and pigeonholed within the memoir genre by an industry unable – or unwilling – to recognize them beyond their perceived status as 'formerly oppressed third-world women'" (Malek, 2006: 364). Thus, stories which validate pre-existing ideas about Iranian women – including works such as *Not Without My Daughter* (Mahmoody, 1991), *Reading Lolita in Tehran: A Memoir in Books* (Nafisi, 2008) and *The Wind in My Hair: My Fight for Freedom in Modern Iran* (Alinejad, 2018) – find particular success as part of a trend in memoirs by women who have "'survived' the Middle East" (Varzi, 2008: para 3).

Interestingly, there seems to be little commercial interest in memoirs written by Iranian men, a tendency no doubt intertwined with the ways in which men of the Middle East are generally constructed as violent and oppressive. Another key set of narratives mobilised to justify wars in Afghanistan and Iraq "contrast[ed] natural and wholesome American male sexuality with abnormal Arab male sexuality [and] . . . innocent and good Americans with evil, violent, savage Arabs" (Jabbra, 2006: 329). Such stereotypes bear on men of the wider Middle East such that, as Varzi points out, Iranian men are often "represented as violent fathers and oppressive husbands, as members of gangs in the European diasporas or as terrorists" (Varzi, 2008: para 17). The cover of *Time* magazine on 9 August 2010 – which featured a young

> Aged 12, myself and other teenage members of my Iranian community group devised a dance performance on the theme of there being no tick box for "Iranian" on ethnicity forms. Assisted by a kind and supportive white British dance teacher, we proclaimed "I am not a tick box; I am not a category; I am my own person" as we rolled about on the floor in draughty community halls across southeast London, holding aloft a series of blow-up globes. At the time, we thought the work was a bit stupid and laughed at how seriously our performance was taken by the adults around us.

Afghan girl whose face had been mutilated on orders of the Taliban under the headline "What Happens If We Leave Afghanistan"[2] – is an example of the ways in which such narratives reproduce colonial imbalances of power: the implication being that if Middle Eastern men are left to their own devices – unsupervised by their white male counterparts – they will inevitably mutilate the women who live amongst them.

Alongside such racialised depictions of Middle Eastern men and women, media narratives which attempt to champion Iranian art and culture – and thus present a "positive" face of Iran – tend to focus on work which excludes or overlooks contemporary Iran and Islam. As Winegar (2008) points out, the selective promotion and display of Middle Eastern art and music in a post-9/11 era favours work that either decontextualises Islam, focusing instead on its ancient "golden age," or erases it, concentrating instead on notions of spiritualism and mysticism. Such a focus has the effect of cementing the pariah status of post-1979 Iran with a concomitant browning effect on people of Iranian heritage since "political constructions of Iran as a deviant, illogical or criminal state are suffused with non-white racialization" (Maghbouleh, 2017: 6). Perhaps unsurprisingly, therefore, many Iranians themselves regularly re-produce discourses which idealise the period of the Persian empire. Such narratives perform a number of functions including: signalling the perceived illegitimacy of the contemporary Islamic Republic; dealing with experiences of "loss of ethnic and cultural

US TRAVEL BAN: CASE STUDIES

British composer must rethink plans for her opera in Pittsburgh

Andrew Ellson
Monday January 30 2017, 12.01am, The Times

Soosan Lolavar, who holds dual British-Iranian citizenship, says the US policy is leading to "very dark places."
    Soosan Lolavar, 29, is having to rethink plans to visit the US next week for rehearsals of an opera she has composed.

Comments (16)

Ali Mostofi
31 JANUARY, 2017
Not one word about the musicians who are locked up and persecuted in Ayatollah prisons.

Dorothy Colston Dachshund
30 JANUARY, 2017
How ironic is it that Britain and America are forced to take in so many political refugees from her country. Iran is no friend of America.

anyfool
30 JANUARY, 2017
Ms Lolavar said: "I feel sad more than anything. I lived in America for a year. It was my home." I lived in China, I am not Chinese. Malaya, I am not Malayan. Germany, I am not German. Gulf States, I am not an Arab. I am not entitled to go to these places, they do not owe me any consideration. If the English were responsible for 99% of world terrorism, I would consider them stupid to allow me an Englishman unfettered

access. Having said that, what could be more stupid than Merkel begging them to come in.

Mr Frank Roby
30 JANUARY, 2017
Soosan Lolavar, Are you British or Iranian? Maybe this is the time to decide.

identity" while living in diaspora (Khakpour, 2014: para 7); distancing oneself from the perceived pariah status of contemporary Iran; and making claims to a white racial identity, "bolstered . . . by cultural mythologies of an ancient, honorable, and dominant Aryan Persian Empire" (Maghbouleh, 2017: 50).

In contemporary context, the non-white status of Iranian communities is particularly evidenced in the difficulties they face in terms of international travel. The surveilling, monitoring, detaining and deporting of Iranian bodies as they attempt to cross international borders reproduces Iranian non-whiteness. As a result, European and American airports have become acute loci of racial Othering for Iranian travellers, which no number of claims to Aryan origins can counter. The global passport index, which lists passports based on their capacity for visa-free travel, ranks the Iranian passport near the bottom in terms of unimpeded movement, at position 194 out of 199.[3] As an example of this positioning, in 2016 the US government instigated a travel ban on citizens from Iran, Iraq, Syria, Libya, Somalia, Sudan and Yemen. (Later, Somalia, Sudan and Iraq were removed from this list and replaced with Venezuela and North Korea.) People of Iranian heritage who are born outside Iran are also subject to certain kinds of travel restrictions. In December 2015, the Visa Waiver Improvement Act blanketly excluded dual citizens of Iran, Iraq, Sudan and Syria (as well as anyone who had travelled to those countries in the previous five years) from the visa waiver programme, which allows citizens of 38 countries to travel to the US, Europe, Japan and South Korea without a visa.

Iranian experiences of race are variegated and complex, intertwining ancient histories of empire with more recent histories of colonialism and discourses of Islamic extremism with stereotypes about oppressive gender relations. While some Iranians continue to make claims to whiteness – as Maghbouleh (2017) notes, however, such claims are, in fact, far less common amongst second-generation Iranian Americans, who tend to articulate the non-white status of Iranians – media narratives of Iranian people and culture alongside travel restrictions and surveillance at airports, effect a browning of Iranian bodies in relation to the assumed majority-white body politic of Europe and North America. I would argue that these forms of Othering experienced by Iranians render them liable to experiences of double-consciousness as raced bodies over whom the effects of colonial discourses linger.

Double-Consciousness and Blackness

While I argue that double-consciousness can be effectively applied to Iranian experiences of Othering in majority-white societies, I am acutely aware of the unique historical lineage of this term, noting particularly the specificity of violent racism that characterises the experience of many Black people in America (which is part of the historical landscape surrounding Du Bois's term). Despite this, it is important to point out that I am not using double-consciousness as a conceptual term to describe racism. Rather, the way I employ it in this book focuses on the internalised feelings of Otherness that arise as a result of living in a racist society: specifically, the sense of fragmentation caused by embodying two ideals which are considered to exist in inherent opposition.

This is not to suggest an equivalence between the varied experiences of Black Americans and my own discussion of British Iranian heritage. The legacy of slavery is a crucial and distinguishing feature of Black diasporic identity, which has specific effects on the form of double-consciousness they embody. The histories of slavery are, fundamentally, not a

EXT. (Exterior) Tehran, a group of people chat outside after the end of a concert, night

FARZAM, Iranian man in his 50s, talks to SOOSAN.

Farzam
So, are you still trying to understand something about Iranian music?

Soosan frowns slightly.

Soosan
Erm . . . well, I did study it with . . .

Farzam
Who?

Soosan
Nima Khaleghi.

Farzam looks disgusted.

Farzam

Oh, so he's recently decided to learn something about Iranian music
then?

Soosan

(Pause) What do you mean?

Farzam

Nima has been catastrophic for Iranian music. He is everything that
is holding Iranian music back. He tries to do it but he just . . . he
doesn't live it.

Soosan

(Hesitant) What do you mean, he doesn't live it?

defining feature of majority Iranian diasporic experience and do not
intersect with my own life.[4] Thus, the kinds of double-consciousness
that inhere in contexts which are relevant to my experience (and
which are the focus of this book) cannot be considered analogous to
the experiences of Black Americans and the original context of this
term.

Furthermore, I consider citation a political tool: a form of memory that
links me to writers in the past, without whom my account could not exist. As Ahmed puts it, citation is "how we acknowledge our debt to those
who came before "(Ahmed, 2017: 15); thus, when I cite Du Bois (1994) –
and, for that matter, Fanon (2008) and Anzaldúa (2012) – I do so not to
suggest that my experiences between and across British and Iranian identities are analogous to those that their work describes. Rather, I aim to
show how it is only through the foundations built by these accounts that
I am able to articulate my experiences at all.

Diaspora

Diaspora is another key term to be explored in this book, and it is to
this concept that I will now turn. Deriving its name from a Greek gar-
dening term referring to the scattering of seeds (Kalra et al., 2005: 9),
classical models of diaspora intertwine histories of forced movement
with exile and loss, particularly focusing on experiences of forced migration amongst Jewish communities from the sixth century BCE and
African peoples as a result of slavery (Kalra et al., 2005: 10). Academic interest in the term began in earnest in the 1990s, and early
definitions underlined the importance of community desire for return
to a literal homeland (Safran, 1991: 83–4 in Clifford, 1994: 304–5).
Subsequently, the African (Gilroy, 1993) and Jewish (Clifford, 1994)

diasporas – thought to be the cases par excellence – have often been found to

> I am sitting in a dressing room waiting to go out onstage, gripping tightly onto the hammers for my santoor. I've only been performing for a year on this instrument, so I feel amateurish and awkward, acutely aware that everyone else is a professional performer. Minutes before we go onstage, I look at Twitter and notice that the organisers of the event have made a short video to promote the concert. I feel a rush of excitement. My name flashes up onscreen, but the image is of a different Iranian musician who looks nothing like me. I can feel myself turning bright red. I mention it to the group, trying my best to remain light-hearted and not look too upset.

lack this emotional pull. Consequently, many writers have de-centred orientation to homeland in their discussions of diaspora, instead favouring a focus on multi-locationality, syncretism and hybridity (Gilroy, 1993; Hall, 1990; Clifford, 1994).

A key aspect of work which de-centres orientation towards homeland is the tendency to view diaspora as a potentially emancipatory discourse in overcoming ethno-nationalism and the strictures of the nation-state. The hope is that diaspora discourse – particularly as explored in the work of Stuart Hall (1990), Paul Gilroy (1993) and James Clifford (1994) – will overcome homogeneous and ethnocentric notions of nationality and identity as part of a broader agenda of humanism and anti-racism (Kalra et al., 2005: 17ff). This is particularly because of the way diaspora offers a means of thinking through identity – and its connection to concepts such as travel and place – that is emergent and untethered to singular nation-states.

It is on this particular point that the framework of diaspora has the potential to reconcile the dislocations of double-consciousness. To reiterate, double-consciousness is an internalised subject-object binary which encourages the individual to look upon themself through the eyes of a hostile and dominant culture. Central to this concept is the inherent tension of embodying two opposing ideals within one human self. In contrast, the frame of diaspora offers a way of thinking through identity that is inherently based on multiplicity. The diasporic subject is constructed as dynamic, syncretic, emergent and tied to multiple places at the same time. We might consider how these aspects of the diaspora frame have the potential to reconcile the fragmentation of double-consciousness by offering a model of identity that moves beyond binary opposition. Ideas of "place" and "travel" are key to this construction, so I will explore first how the concept of diaspora disrupts ethno-nationalist discourses of place and second how it retrieves emancipatory discourses of travel for diasporic subjects.

Disrupting Ethno-nationalist Discourses of Place

A key potential of the discourse of diaspora is its capacity to disrupt the notion that ethno-nationalist identities are necessarily tied to singular geographical places. This not only questions the assumption that cultural belonging refers to a unitary location but also

Parisa (V.O.)

Pretty rarely.

Soosan stands up.

Soosan

Is it so rare? I think we react to it really differently; you don't mind people telling you your name is weird.

Parisa (V.O.)

Because people are dumb and lazy. I've been called the wrong name for ten years at work; you just have to deal with it.

Soosan

I told you that I think people asking intrusive questions about my Dad is dog-whistle Islamophobia, and you told me I was being ridiculous.

Parisa (V.O.)

I didn't say you were being ridiculous, and I'm not saying those things don't come from ignorance. It's just you get really upset about them, and I think sometimes you just have to let things go a bit.

Soosan sits down, rests her head in her hand.

Soosan

(Pause) Aren't you on the BAME group at work? How can you be on that if you identify as white?

destabilises the primacy of the nation-state in such discussions. As Clifford puts it, diasporic attachments traverse or subvert "the nation-state as common territory and time" (Clifford, 1994: 307), exploring alternate public spheres and articulating

> ways to stay and be different, to be British *and something else* complexly related to Africa and the Americas, to shared histories of enslavement, racist subordination, cultural survival, hybridization, resistance, and political rebellion.
>
> (Clifford, 1994: 308)

At the same time, this model de-centres the west in narratives of social organisation, "recovering non-Western, or not-only-Western, models for cosmopolitan life" (Clifford, 1994: 328).

Gilroy's (1993) seminal study of the Black diaspora similarly argues that diasporic encounters disrupt ethno-nationalist claims. By foregrounding "histories of crossing, migration, exploration, interconnection, and travel – forced and voluntary" (Clifford, 1994: 316), Gilroy highlights the syncretism of Black culture, formed in flow between the Americas, Europe and

> Since I got back from Iran, I have felt intensely anxious. I am highly emotional, often on the verge of tears for most of the day, and my behaviour has become weird and at times oddly compulsive. I'm struck and annoyed by the increasing *whiteness* of Brixton. I find myself seeking out brown people, trying to get away from the mono-culture. I feel an intense sense of loss of identity, not sure who I am or where I fit.

Africa. The hybrid creole forms of music that are produced out of this "disorganic formation" (Gilroy, 1993: 122) are characterised by "doubleness, their unsteady location simultaneously inside and outside conventions" (Gilroy, 1993: 73).

Stuart Hall further elaborates on the hybrid nature of diasporic cultures with particular reference to post-colonial migrations between the UK and Caribbean. He contends that the diaspora experience is

> defined, not by essence or purity, but by the recognition of a necessary heterogeneity and diversity; by a conception of "identity" which lives with and through, not despite, difference; by *hybridity*.
>
> (Hall, 1990: 235, emphasis in original)

Hall's construction of diasporic identity as emergent, contingent and changing has the effect of further problematising ethno-nationalist claims to purity and belonging.

The works of Clifford (1994), Gilroy (1993) and Hall (1990) all serve to problematise connections between place and belonging which tie identities to singular geographical places. Instead, they offer a model of selfhood wherein identity is not a fixed thing but, rather, a dynamic state of becoming within which syncretism plays a central role. This aspect of the diaspora frame has particular potential to reconcile the psychological fragmentation of double-consciousness wherein the self is experienced as split between opposing ideals. Indeed, in my own experience, and for many years, I have conceived of my self as split between dichotomous identities

I really miss Iran. I miss being around and amongst Iranian people. But at the same time, Iran is exhausting; being there really depletes me, and all this hits me when I come back. I felt like I had to oppress so much of myself when I was there, not responding to strange comments either because it wasn't worth it or because I don't always have the linguistic skills. Whether it's my cousin commenting on how I should blow dry my hair or wear more makeup; my aunt describing me as "very strange" because I spent so much time studying Farsi; how several people described me as soft, gentle, which stands so far away from my own self-image such a lot of biting my tongue, passively watching while people talk *about* me when I am standing right there in front of them. It seems that many of those emotions are flooding out of me now, uncontrolled and at great speed. All this weighs on me heavily – the weight of their ideas about who I am as well as my own lack of energy in confronting their (mis) conceptions.

Whenever I try to explain the ways I feel restricted in Iran, people reply that it must be hard living in and then returning from such an oppressive country. Eventually, I stop bothering to correct them when they say this.

I feel lost. I am in an in-between space from which I cannot escape.

labelled as British and Iranian. That these identities are experienced as separate, fixed and tied to singular geographical places has caused me to feel intense internal fragmentation and a sense of being unfulfilled. In contrast, the frame of diaspora offers a model of identity fundamentally based on multi-locationality and syncretism, valuing the very kinds of hybridity that have for many years left me feeling incomplete. Perhaps this emancipatory model could offer a pathway towards reconciling these experiences and finding a new way of conceiving of my hybrid self.

However, some commentators have questioned the extent to which the multi-locationality of the diaspora frame offers an emancipatory model of identity. This is particularly important when considering the extent to which the forces of coloniality play an important role in pushing and pulling diasporic subjects in certain directions. If the frame of diaspora merely reinscribes colonial power dynamics – rather than stepping beyond them through a model of multi-locationality – then perhaps the paradigm of identity it offers fails to live up to its emancipatory potential.

Many diaspora communities are formed of those migrating from (formerly) colonised nations towards the colonial "centre." The reasons for doing so are varied and complex but certainly include a desire to seek prosperity, peace and opportunity, which colonial imbalances of power may have rendered difficult to find in their "home" nations. Perhaps unsurprisingly, therefore, scholarly writing on diaspora largely emanates from diasporic voices in elite western-based academic centres whose routes to such locations tend to intertwine with histories of colonial subjecthood. Spivak (1988, 1999) views such processes as a form of neo-Orientalism, in which academic work raises diasporic hybridity over native experience,

Chris Sones chris.sones@bbc.co.uk

Tue, Mar 12, 2019, 1:42 PM

Dear Soosan

Forgive me, I'm not sure if you are still resident in this country. But . . .

As a follow up to the conference on diversity in composition that we organised a couple of years ago, we at Radio 3 along with our partners at BASCA and the RNCM, are putting together a workshop with a select group of representatives from the classical music industry, and with composers, to explore the workings of a new initiative we have for increasing diversity in classical composition and foregrounding and promoting composers from a BAME background. The workshop will be half a day in Manchester *on 1st May*, from lunchtime at the RNCM.

We are keen to explore the experiences and possible obstacles composers encounter establishing their careers in this country and to try to understand how best to counter these obstacles. The workshop is by invitation only. Might you be free/interested in being one of our participants?

Very best wishes

Chris Sones – Producer BBC R3

highlighting utterances of the global centre over the silenced voices of the global south (Spivak, 1999: 168–9). As Hutnyk (2005: 97) succinctly puts it, Spivak argues that "hybridized and diasporized members of the cosmopolitan set [market] themselves as representatives of the culture they call origin from the luxurious comfort they now call home."

Indeed, it could be argued that the centre of intellectual research on diaspora (or, for that matter, in general) remains located in the global north, and experiences of migrancy and diaspora as they relate to scholarship recreate a largely centripetal movement towards the most prestigious academic jobs, the majority of archives and the primary language of scholarship. As a result, many intellectuals of the global south are unable to speak their native languages in a scholarly way, rendering them "especially susceptible to . . . coming westward" (John, 1989: 71).

With this mind it might be argued that, rather than producing an emancipatory model of

Farzam

He's not inside it; he doesn't know anything about it. He doesn't know what real Iranian music is.

Soosan shifts uncomfortably.

Soosan

But . . . he studied Iranian music for many years. He knows—

Farzam

He doesn't know anything about real Iranian music. He doesn't know its soul; he just stands outside it. His work has been really . . . (pause) It's been catastrophic.

Soosan

I don't really understand what you're saying.

Farzam

It's like you. You speak Persian, but you're not really Persian, are you? People like you and Nima, you are looking at the culture from the outside; you're not really part of it, are you? You're not really a part of all this (gestures around him). Do you think your music is really Persian?

Soosan looks down while going increasingly red

Soosan

Well, I mean, I do use things in my pieces . . . like in that piece . . .

Farzam

Ah yes. Look, I really want to talk to you more about that piece of yours. I'd really like to take you for a coffee sometime so we can talk about it more, in more detail. Because I can see that you're very (long pause) serious about it. I can tell that you *want* to understand. But you're looking at it from the outside; you're not really living it, are you?

FADE OUT.

identity based on multi-locationality, the diaspora frame reproduces a magnetic pull towards former colonial centres, in turn reinscribing colonialist imbalances of power. According to this view, as long as native informants emplaced in the global north speak for and about a global south which remains distant and unknowable, the syncretism of diasporic identity cannot really be claimed as emancipatory. This conflict is crucial to discussions of double-consciousness, itself an internalised subject-object binary in which the individual looks upon themself through the eyes of a hostile, dominant and racist culture. Central to this experience is a conflict between the normative majority culture and non-normative subaltern form, constructions which are often entangled with colonialist histories. These tensions within the concept of diaspora will provide the material basis for further exploration of this frame, with particular focus on the extent to which it can reconcile the fragmentation of double-consciousness. This will be explored through compositions entitled *Tradition-Hybrid-Survival* and *I Am the Spring, You Are the Earth* in Chapter 4.

Emancipatory Discourses of Travel

A second important aspect of the diaspora frame is its entanglement with emancipatory discourses of travel. It might be suggested that by accounting for travel by diasporic subjects outside the binary logic of colonialism, this frame has the potential to reconcile the psychological fragmentation of double-consciousness. This counters an internalised sense of the self as split between two opposing ideals, with a self that is emergent and – through routes of travel – has the potential to grow and change.

"Travel" is a highly racialised and gendered term, such that travel in the adventurous, ennobling, heroic sense is overwhelmingly associated with white western men (Clifford, 1997: 31; Wolff, 1993). As Clifford notes, white women travellers, particularly in the late 19th century, "were forced to conform, masquerade, or rebel discreetly within a set of normatively

                              Parisa (V.O.)
Because I foreground the ways in which my life experience is on the basis of being treated as white while also acknowledging that I have heritage which allows me to be on that group. And when I said this to my Black colleagues on the council they, said they were really pleased to hear that – that it's good to hear someone admit that privilege and not try and claim that all BAME experiences are the same. I think I can sit on that council, but I have to be really clear about my life experience, which is as a passing person.

Soosan looks confused.

                              Soosan
Well, look, if you say that you *identify* as a white person, then aren't you a hypocrite to sit on a council for minority ethnic people?

                              Parisa (V.O.)
No, because I'm not saying I *am* white; I'm saying I get treated as if I'm white the majority of the time.

Soosan stands up and start pacing the room while talking animatedly.

Soosan

This is what I don't get. How can we be BAME in one moment and then not in another? And why is everything based on other people's thoughts and perceptions; why is it all about whether we pass or not? Why does that define our identity? I just think defining your entire self on the basis of how other people perceive you is just so narrow and depressing. It means that there is no core sense of me. And this is exactly what happened in my childhood. I had no sense of myself whatsoever outside of what people told me I was. When people in Iranian school told me I was really English, I went along with that; when people at school asked where I was from, I had to explain that I was Iranian. I was constantly responding to what other people thought I was. There was no inner stability. And this whole idea of whiteness comes from my Dad and Iranians thinking they're white, which is completely made up. They're not. They only said that to define themselves as better than Arabs.

Parisa laughs.

You can identify however you want, and I get that this whole thing is weird and confusing and messy. I'm not saying I identify as someone who has been oppressed, and to be honest, I don't know exactly how I identify, but "white" is not the right word any more, and I want a sense of myself that comes from me, that is stable and central to who I am and doesn't change depending on what someone on the street might assume of me.

male definitions and experiences" (Clifford, 1997: 32). Similarly, non-white bodies are often kept out of discourses of noble travel, such that "in the dominant discourses of travel, a non-white person cannot figure as a heroic explorer" (Clifford, 1997: 33).

Gilroy's (1993) work explicitly aims to recover routes of travel for Black people that are not entirely wrapped up in trauma. He posits a tendency amongst histories of migration to consider the movement of Black subjects largely through frameworks of travel as coerced

I have consistently struggled to have any sense of my *being Iranian* as part of a differential becoming or iterative intra-activity in which I am inherently involved, and instead have consistently constructed it as something that exists in a complete form outside me, which I can either succeed or fail in apprehending. My life experiences have centred on the idea of "Iranianness" as an object or thing that I perceive from afar which I am able to look upon from a variety of different positions. There are

and violent and concomitantly disconnected from understandings of travel as recreational or aspirational (Gilroy, 1993: 133). This, in turn, produces Black travel as largely a process of loss and despair, overlooking the ways in which such processes can act as mechanisms for self-betterment, creativity and the production of new hybrid cultural forms. More broadly, this focus disrupts discourses within which the theatre of the global south is sustained by narratives of "survival" or "escape."

The ways in which discourses of travel preclude particular bodies from certain kinds of mobility are eminently relevant to the production of knowledge. As Clifford suggests (1989), there is a deep connection between travel and theory, such that '"theory" is a product of

Parisa (V.O.)

Yeah, but that opinion of someone on the street – which is probably that you are white – that is really important. Whiteness is privilege. Whiteness is not thinking about race. Whiteness is just blending in, being normal. You know that TV programme you told me to watch? Well, that girl talked about how she knew when she was little that to be white was to be beautiful. And she used to ask her mum why she wasn't whiter, why *she* couldn't be beautiful. Did you ever feel that way? (pause) And when she was choosing which room to go in, I really think we would have had more in common with the white group. Don't you?

Soosan sighs.

Anyway, the fact that you are just thinking about this now in your 30s shows that the politics of race hasn't affected your whole life. You and I have the luxury that we can out ourselves if we like, or we can choose not to for our own safety. I understand what you're saying, but I think it's important that we don't try and claim something that doesn't belong to us. (Pause) I think what I'm trying to say is you don't need to co-opt the language of Otherness just to find meaning in yourself.

Soosan leans back on the sofa and looks up at the ceiling.

FADE OUT.

displacement, comparison, a certain distance. To theorize, one leaves home" (Clifford, 1989: 177). Characteristics of travel associated with white western men – as brave, adventurous, dangerous and ennobling – surely also relate to the image of the courageous traveller-theorist striking out on their own in the intellectual wilderness. This raises questions about what kinds of bodies are able to theorise, echoing Spivak's (1988) contention that practices of neo-colonialism render the subaltern unable to produce their own theoretical practices. As she presents it, the ideal agent of scholarly research remains white, male and positioned in the global north, underlining non-white bodies as the Other to theoretical practices.

When considering travel as a process with emancipatory potential, it is important to remember – once again – that many of these theoretical discussions emanate from academic voices based in Europe and the United States. This includes figures such as Gilroy (UK), Clifford (US) and Hall (who was born in Jamaica but lived his adult life in the UK). Indeed, academic communities are inherently transnational and mobile; therefore, the very people producing theories of mobility are those with very privileged experiences of such a process (Schwalgin, 2004: 76).

Moreover, it is pertinent to recognise the ways in which questions of freedom of movement often linger in such discussions. One could ask, "How can you access the emancipatory potential of travel if you are an inmate interned in Guantanamo bay or a South Asian labourer working under the kafala system in Qatar?"[5] As Sharma (1996: 18) points out, co-opting discourses of travel as emancipatory renders invisible the "violence endemic in the production of migrancy." This means that the migrant is decontextualised as a

> times when I feel I can "see" the object-like form of my Iranianness with clarity, and in these moments, I am less aware of barriers standing in the way. There are others when the glass through which I apprehend this object is so cracked and splintered that the form of it is completely distorted, and I feel ashamed and lost. Indeed, I consider myself as existing in a state of constant movement in relationship to the object-like form of my Iranianness – sometimes considering it from very close, at others alienated from it to the point where it almost disappears. And yet, at all times, the form of the object remains delineated, distinct and static; it is only the positioning of me, the subject, which shifts and moves around it or my view of the object which fragments. In this way, my perceiving body is alienated from the object-like form of my Iranianness and afforded only the ability to look upon it from a distance.

"transcendental subject of subalternity . . . outside the workings of contemporary neo-colonialism." Within such debates, there is a danger that attempts to retrieve travel as an emancipatory process for diasporic subjects de-centres histories of violence which both undergird and restrict much diasporic migration. These ideas will be discussed in more detail with particular reference to the composition *Tradition-Hybrid-Survival*.

Drawing on the positions outlined here, I posit a working definition of the emancipatory frame of diaspora as:

> *A frame which theorises transnational communities and cultures, particularly through the lens of travel and place. It offers a means of considering identity that is syncretic, emergent and dynamic, as*

well as untethered to a singular nation-state. It also aims to retrieve a framework of travel for diasporic subjects that stands outside pain and despair. However, due to the

In June 2017, I attended an Iranian American Women's Foundation event in London. A London-based Iranian charity gave me a free ticket, and since the event had a focus on women in the arts, I decided to go along. I was incredibly nervous about attending – so much so that I couldn't quite make myself leave the house for hours. In the end, I didn't get to the event till 3pm, despite the fact that it started at 9:30 in the morning. I hadn't eaten lunch, so I was light-headed and exhausted.

I have never felt more uncomfortable and out of place at a conference in my life, not only because everyone in the room seemed hugely wealthy – the tickets cost £300 each – but they were also so *Iranian*. I looked at the people around me and then at myself in the mirror, wondering if I looked Iranian enough to be here. I became irrationally obsessed with the idea that someone might ask me to leave. I also looked a mess. I was in jeans and trainers, and my hair was all over the place while the other women appeared very glamourous in body-con dresses, heels and suits. I hastily put on some more makeup in the loo and tried to push my hair into some sort of shape, hoping that this might help in some way.

In a break between sessions, all the women filed into an atrium to have tea and biscuits and mingle with other attendees. I overheard somebody proclaim: "I'm not your average Iranian woman; I'm very daring." I saw someone I know – a friendly French Iranian pianist I met in Pittsburgh – but I was so overcome with awkwardness that I couldn't go over and speak to her. Instead, I left the atrium and sat on a sofa around the corner by myself, eating a pastry and pretending to look through the conference booklet. I felt like a complete idiot.

The final panel took place in a large ballroom filled with circular tables and hundreds of seats all facing towards a brightly lit stage where the conference organiser introduced us to the "next generation" of Iranian women. Before the panel, the organiser – a well-groomed Iranian American women in her 40s wearing a smart dress – asked us to applaud all the men who had come to the conference. I didn't applaud. She then introduced the four young women sitting on stage by saying, "Don't let their good looks fool you; they have accomplished a lot."

fact that diasporic migrations are crucially impacted by colonial imbalances of power and that such routes are overwhelmingly theorised from the position of elite voices located in the global north, this frame can be charged with de-centring the politics of coloniality and presenting an apolitical construction of travel as undifferentiated mobility which obscures the potential violence of migrancy.

By presenting a model of identity that is multi-locational, syncretic, emergent and responsive to travel-as-growth, the diaspora frame may have the potential to contribute to a reconciliation of the psychological fragmentation of double-consciousness which I experience.

Reflections

This chapter has juxtaposed multiple texts, often overlapping them in ways that disrupt the flow of the narrative and force the reader to move backwards and forwards while reading. This structure draws attention to the ways in which scholarly and personal narratives intertwine, at times connecting and following each other, at others diverging or opening up new and distinct paths.

The scholarly voice in this chapter tends towards the singular, objective and empirical, offering a conventional view-from-nowhere account. The embodied texts – encompassing diary entries, experiential vignettes, screenplays, email correspondence and real-life news clippings – offer a more personal, complex and nuanced account of the concepts of diaspora and double-consciousness. The *juxtaposition* of these texts attempts to draw links between these two distinct voices, offering a fractious story which starts and stops and includes some aspects which contradict each other or do not connect in an obvious way.

It is in the complex relationship *between* texts that the role of the reader comes to the fore, encouraging them to make links between what might seem to be disconnected narratives and uncover the meanings that exist amongst the various parts being presented. This process attempts to pull the reader back into the text, manoeuvring them away from the role of detached observer which is a potential outcome of their reading either an analytical or personal text in isolation. Crucially, this encourages the reader to experience the text not as a series of delineated objects from which they are alienated but, rather, as a series of *materials* with which they must correspond to ascertain meaning. Thus, the form of this text resists passive reading since the reader is forced to move backwards and forwards in order to retain the sense of what is being said. It also enables the reader to experience a *sense* of the psychic splitting which is inherent in the concept of double-consciousness. Of course, an arrangement of texts on a page can only be considered a *caricature* of an intensely painful sense of internal dislocation which the concept of double-consciousness describes. Even so, this means of representing the concepts of diaspora and double-consciousness (accompanied by the next chapter which explores my life experience in more detail) gestures towards the very kinds of performative, embodied knowledge which are central to my exploration of these terms.

Notes

1 Where appropriate, names have been changed to protect identities.
2 http://content.time.com/time/magazine/0,9263,7601100809,00.html (last accessed 4 July 2020).
3 www.passportindex.org/byIndividualRank.php?ccode=ir (last accessed 2 July 2020).
4 While it is true that majority Iranianness is not intimately entangled with slavery in the way that Black American identity is, it is important to note that there is a significant Afro-Iranian minority community in the southern provinces of Iran whose ancestry can include histories of enslavement. The history of such communities is long and complex (with some suggestion that they date back to the 9th century CE) but crucially includes a period in the 15th and 16th centuries when Portuguese traders transported enslaved people originally from Somalia and Zanzibar to the Iranian coast (Varahram, 2015). While there are few official statistics on the number of Afro-Iranians, these groups have come to increased prominence due to the work of photo-journalists documenting the existence of such communities (www.theguardian.com/world/gallery/2015/apr/30/irans-forgotten-african-migrants-in-pictures) and public advocacy groups which amplify the voices of Black Iranians in the diaspora (https://collectiveforblackiranians.org).
5 www.theguardian.com/global-development/2020/sep/01/new-employment-law-effectively-ends-qatars-exploitative-kafala-system.

4 Diaspora, Wayfaring and Transport

> Last night, I had a dream I was playing santoor. It was a dark room, and I was sitting on the floor. Something else was happening as part of the per-formance – was it dance? Kae? I couldn't see; it was so dimly lit. I could barely make out the edges of the instrument, but I could sense a ring of people around me, waiting patiently for the performance to begin. I struck the santoor, and immediately a string broke. I hit it again, and another snapped in two. With every strike, something shattered: a string twanged into the air; a piece of wood splintered. With every hammer, some new part broke off and flew at me, sometimes hitting me in the face. I kept hammering away regardless, watching the whole thing gradually fall to pieces with my every stroke. After not much time, all that was left was a mess of wood and wire on the floor. I held the hammers limply in my hand and felt hundreds of eyes staring at me expectantly in the darkness.
>
> (Personal diary, 12 June 2019)

For many years, exploration of ideas connected with Iranian music has been a key part of my practice as a musician. This work has taken a great many forms, including work for Iranian and western instruments/players (*Only Sound Remains*, 2013; *Inventory of My Life*, 2018; *I Am the Spring, You Are the Earth*, 2019); pieces exploring melodic or rhythmic ideas de-rived from Iranian music (*Set Your Life on Fire*, 2015; *Mah Didam*, 2016; *Girl*, 2017); pieces exploring tuning systems derived from Iranian music (*Every Strand of Thread and Rope*, 2023); and work exploring issues of travel, place, dislocation and memory (*ID, Please*, 2017; *Golha*, 2019). As noted previously, I found working in this way to be at once exciting and challenging for my practice as a musician and deeply complex for me as a person. This is because of the ways in which epistemologies of music composition – making and moving with sound – opened up ways of knowing about diaspora, Otherness and double-consciousness that had otherwise remained unknowable through other means. Working in this way forced me to confront aspects of my life that had lain dormant

DOI: 10.4324/9781003351450-4

for many years. This experience is depicted in the earlier quote, recalling a dream I had after the third performance of *Inventory of My Life*,[1] whose imagery of splitting and breaking also reflects the fragmentation of double-consciousness.

Despite this broad variety of work, only two compositions will form the basis of the analysis in this book: a work for cello and string ensemble called *Tradition-Hybrid-Survival* and a piece for improvising ensemble called *I Am the Spring, You Are the Earth*. In particular, I explore the framework of diaspora against the backdrop of deep reflection on my life experiences entangled with ways of working with sound in the context of these particular pieces. This will enable me to consider the effectiveness of the diaspora metaphor in reconciling the psychological fragmentation of double-consciousness as I experience it. To reiterate, the frame of diaspora, particularly as it is presented by writers like Gilroy (1993), Clifford (1994) and Hall (1990), offers a way of thinking through identity that is inherently based on multiplicity, through which the diasporic subject is constructed as dynamic, syncretic, emergent and tied to multiple places at the same time. We might consider how these aspects of the diaspora frame have the potential to reconcile the fragmentation of double-consciousness by offering a model of identity that moves beyond binary opposition and towards a dynamic state of becoming.

Ideas of "place" and "travel" are key to this construction, so in order to consider the frame of diaspora, I will further interrogate these essential components. My question here is: what would it mean in the context of diaspora theory to move away from a theory of place as based on fixed and bounded destinations? How could diaspora effectively take account of the fact that lives are lived through and around places, not *in* them? How might we conceive of the idea that people are not static occupants but, rather, inhabitants who are always on their way to someplace else? In short, how might the concept of diaspora be energised or transfigured when explored through the lens of Ingold's notion of "wayfaring" and its counter, which he terms "transport" (Ingold, 2007, 2008)?

Wayfaring and Transport

Tim Ingold's metaphor of wayfaring offers a means of understanding ideas of both place and travel. He posits that place is not simply an empty locus that exists in the world, but rather a dynamic notion that is brought into being by the function of human and non-human movement along the world. That is to say, place is not a priori delineated and defined, rather it is the continual movement of activity that brings the idea of place to life. Key to Ingold's argument is the notion that "human existence . . . unfolds not in places but along paths" (Ingold, 2008: 33). Indeed, human life is not enclosed within defined areas but is instead constantly moving and wending its way amongst a dynamic landscape. For Ingold, it is the trails left by this ongoing movement along the world that bring the very idea of place into being. As a result, ideas of place are in a constant state of becoming, gradually emerging as inhabitants pass along the world (see Figure 4.1).

Ingold's model further encourages us to perceive of places as interconnected by the ongoing dynamic movement of subjects along them. That is to say, while on the trail, the inhabitant is always *somewhere*, but each somewhere is always on its way to (and from) somewhere else (Ingold, 2008: 34). These trails do not remain singular and distinct. As the lives of inhabitants meet, their trails are intertwined, forming a knot of entanglements which stretch beyond in multiple directions. When a great number of these entanglements come together, they form a meshwork of interwoven and completely knotted strands. As such, Ingold conceives of place not as "a nexus within which all life, growth and activity are *contained*" (Ingold, 2007: 96) but rather as knots formed from the entanglement of the varied trails along which human existence unfolds. He describes the state of progressing along such trails as "wayfaring," Paul Klee's famous description of the line which "goes out for a walk" (Klee, 1961: 105 in Ingold, 2007: 73) encapsulates the way that the trails of the wayfarer are dynamic and develop freely in time (see Figure 4.2).

Ingold's concept of wayfaring produces an understanding of travel as dynamic and, crucially, ongoing. That is to say, the wayfarer is always

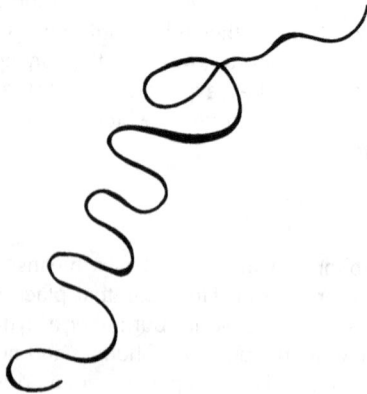

Figure 4.1 A perambulatory trail

Source: Ingold, 2007: 72

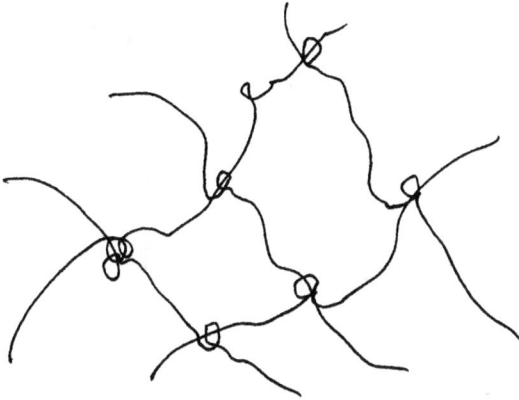

Figure 4.2 A meshwork of knotted trails
Source: Ingold, 2008: 38

moving along the world, progressing along pathways whose inscription brings the notion of place into being. As a result, the travel of wayfaring eschews the idea of a moment of "arrival" at a destination, since this requires the wayfarer to be "in place" at one time and "out of place" at another. Ideas of destination and arrival are more closely aligned with In-gold's contrasting analogy of travel and place which he terms "transport" and to which I will now turn.

In contrast to the dynamic, entangled and unfolding nature of wayfar-ing, transport offers a fixed and destination-oriented notion of place and movement. If the trail of wayfaring is winding, reactive and experientially unfolding, the line of transport moves directly from point to point between specific nodes or destinations which are pinned down by the lines which connect them (Ingold, 2008: 37) (see Figure 4.3).

Whereas wayfaring "takes us on a journey that has no obvious be-ginning or end," transport "presents us with an array of interconnected destinations that can, as on a route-map, be viewed all at once" (Ingold, 2007: 73). Furthermore, rather than playing an active and unfolding role in the creation of paths which then become entangled in knots and mesh-works of place, the passenger of transport is "temporarily exiled whilst in transit" (Ingold, 2007: 77) and remains in this state until they reach their destination or port of re-entry *into* the world. Thus, the body of the passenger is alienated from processes of movement, since they do not move themselves but rather are *moved* from place to place. In Paul Klee's language, the line of transport is "more like a series of appointments than a walk" (Klee, 1961: 109 in Ingold, 2007: 73). Or as Ingold describes it, "it goes from point to point, in sequence, as quickly as possible, and in

Figure 4.3 A series of nodes pinned down by the lines that connect them
Source: Ingold, 2007: 74

principle in no time at all, for every successive destination is already fixed prior to setting out" (Ingold, 2007: 73).

   Crucially, wayfaring describes the essentials of human and non-human existence in the world, while pure transport (despite its prevalence as an analogy) is essentially a fallacy. As Ingold puts it, "we cannot get from location to location by leap-frogging the world, nor can we the traveller ever be quite the same on arrival at a place as when we set out" (Ingold, 2007: 10). Here, we may note a crucial link between the ideas of wayfaring and transport and the concepts of performative and constative epistemologies. Both wayfaring and performative research methods recognise that all of human and non-human existence is lived in direct material engagement with the world, and thus, you cannot step out of bodily engagement with that world via processes of travel or the act of theorising. By contrast, transport and constative processes reproduce the notion that the traveller/theorist can step out of the world either to observe it or to undertake a process of travel in order to "arrive" at a new destination.

Realities of Travel and Place

Despite its theoretical efficacy, Ingold's notions of place and travel can overshadow certain realities of such processes. Even though his model is not explicitly about large-scale, international travel (he talks about moving around one's own house as an example of wayfaring), the question of access remains due to the fact that a minimum degree of autonomy and freedom of movement is required to be "always on one's way to some place else." As noted previously, one could ask how you can access the emancipatory potential of such a model of place and travel if you are interned in a refugee camp.

Ingold's constructions of travel and place share with the emancipatory frame of diaspora a potential issue noted previously. This refers to their tendency to *(de-centre) the politics of coloniality and (present) an apolitical construction of travel as undifferentiated mobility which obscures the potential violence of migrancy.* I recognise the pitfalls of utilising such a model to explore the emancipatory frame of diaspora, with particular reference to its potential to double down on some of these issues.

And yet, I argue that it is still of value to superimpose these frames, largely due to the fact that the aim of this project is to interrogate the emancipatory frame of diaspora, *specifically as a means for reconciling the fragmentation of double-consciousness.* In order to explore such ideas, I have produced a highly personal exploration of my own experiences across identities labelled as British and Iranian, and these experiences are simply not defined by the kind of violence or danger which could be erased by both the emancipatory models of diaspora or Ingold's notions of place and travel.

There is no doubt that lingering power balances of colonialism – alongside questions of gender, money and social status – played an important role in my father moving to the UK to study in the 1960s. It is also clear that my experiences of double-consciousness have been characterised by confusion for much of my life. But it is certainly not the case that – to quote the work *Home* by Somali-British poet Warsan Shire[2] – my father left home because home was the "mouth of a shark," nor that I have experienced the physical "violence of migrancy" as Sharma (1996: 18) and others described it. Indeed, stories of migration are multitudinous, varied and complex, and a framework that can usefully explore one kind of diasporic experience may erase the specificity of another. Therefore, while Ingold's model of travel and place has been hugely productive in exploring the concepts of double-consciousness and diaspora from the vantage point of my own experiences, such a model may erase the specificity of narratives of travel and migrancy more tightly bound up with violence.

I will now consider what nuance can be added to the emancipatory frame of diaspora by exploring it through the lens of wayfaring/transport alongside ideas of travel and place. To do so, I will consider two of my compositions – *Tradition-Hybrid-Survival* and *I Am the Spring, You Are the Earth.* Specifically, I will explore the ways in which *Tradition-Hybrid-Survival* reproduces the metaphor of transport, while also containing some elements which lend themselves to the frame of wayfaring. In contrast, *I Am the Spring, You Are the Earth* fits more squarely within the wayfaring framework.

Tradition-Hybrid-Survival

I have endeavoured as much as possible to write the following section with a non-specialist audience in mind. As part of such an aim, I describe particular musical processes through text-based descriptions, depictions of sections of the score and targeted clips from recordings. The two pieces which are the focus of this book are publicly available. *Tradition-Hybrid-Survival* is on the 2024 album *Girl* conducted by Kelly Lovelady, performed by Ruthless Jabiru and on the label *Nonclassical*. *I Am the Spring, You Are the Earth* is on the 2019 album *Stepping Back, Jumping In* by Laura Jurd and on the label *Edition Records*. I indicate which section of each recording to listen to in the text. I strongly encourage the reader to listen to the music described while reading this book. The text-based discussions contained here tell only part of the story, and it is only through combining this with experience of the sounding music that my argument can be fully grasped.

Tradition-Hybrid-Survival is a 20-minute concerto for solo cello and string ensemble that premiered in London in 2018.[3] The programme note gives a brief background to the process of conceiving and composing the piece:

> I wrote this piece during a period when I was travelling a great deal between the UK and Iran and had to constantly re-make myself as I moved between these very different places. Most often when visiting my family in Tehran, I feel like a strange mixture of British and Iranian, a member of the Iranian diaspora visiting from abroad. But there are many times when I misunderstand what is going on or find myself in an unfamiliar situation and feel completely lost; a total outsider. Equally, there are some rare occurrences when shopping with my aunt or drinking tea with my family when I feel fleetingly and momentarily like I have come home. In these instances I have a deep sense that Iran is a special place where a unique part of me lives.

Drawing on these experiences of feeling pulled between identity groupings, the string ensemble is divided into groups labelled "local," "diaspora" and "outsider" (see Figure 4.4). The local group represent persons of common cultural heritage who are co-present and whose actions are directed into greater alignment through the sharing of a locality and its concomitant laws, practices, codes and customs. They explore material in the tonal centre of G and form the largest group, gathered in the centre

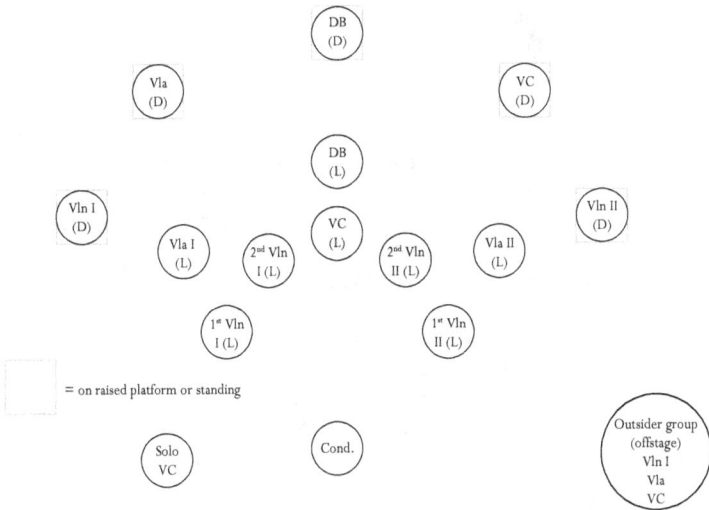

Figure 4.4 Layout of ensemble showing positioning of local (L), diaspora (D) and outsider groups

of the stage. They are defined musically by working collectively as a unit with limited individual divergence.

The diaspora group represents people of shared cultural heritage who are separated in space and time. They are physically distinct from the local group through their positioning onstage since they either stand or sit on a raised platform behind them. Similarly, they are somewhat distanced from each other since they are positioned in one curved line rather than grouped together as a standard string section. Their material exists in the tonal centres of both G and B, and they have slightly more of a sense of individuality than the local players.

The final group amongst the ensemble are the outsiders. They represent vague and distant Others: people who drop in from nowhere and then disappear again just as quickly. They are unseen, unconducted and virtually unknown to the wider group since they are physically separate from the rest of the ensemble and explore musical material which operates entirely independently from anything else in the piece. Their material exists entirely in the tonal centre of B, and they are positioned offstage, choosing their own tempo when playing and responding to vague instructions about when to begin and end.

As indicated in Figure 4.4, which shows how the performers are spatially arranged, spatialisation plays a key role in *Tradition-Hybrid-Survival.*

From the second half of the twentieth century onwards, spatialisation became a prominent concern for many composers who recognised the potential to unlock new possibilities of musical narrative and experience by organising musical elements in physical space. For early pioneers such as Karlheinz Stockhausen, space was considered a hitherto neglected aspect of sound that could be serialised in much the same way as pitch or timbre. As he wrote in relation to his work *Hymnen* (1966–7), "[T]he direction and movement of sounds . . . is as important in this work as melody, harmony, rhythm, dynamic, colour and semantic." Thus in this early period, he considered the spatial dimension an extension of his broader processes of total serialism (Stockhausen, 1991: 91).

Iannis Xenakis drew on his background as an architect to explore architectural space in many of his compositions. His work *Terretektorh* (1965) attempts to sonically recreate the shape of a spiral through dispersing performers amongst the audience. *Metastaseis* (1953–4) uses en masse string glissandi to evoke a hyperbolic paraboloid, a shape famously reproduced in the Philips Pavilion built by Xenakis and Le Corbusier and featuring music by Edgard Varèse for the Expo 58 in Brussels (Xenakis and Kanach, 2008: 95). For Luigi Nono, spatialisation was inherently linked to theatre and political activism by using this element of sound as a way to create a new kind of listening. As he writes, his aim was to "wake up the ear, the eyes, human thinking, intelligence" in order to affect a political awakening amongst the audience (Nono, 2001: 522).

In *Tradition-Hybrid-Survival*, spatialisation is used as a means of dramatising and critically reflecting on cultural processes, particularly as they relate to the concept of diaspora. Specifically, it helps give clear definition to the three identity groups and their relationships to one another. For example, the outsiders attain their Otherness by their location offstage, the local group are positioned closest to the audience and at the centre of the work, while the diaspora orbit them at a small distance. Thus, the way that each group is positioned in the space helps construct who they are within the narrative of the work. Similarly, spatialisation allows sound to travel between and across groups, particularly the diaspora and local groups, who share much musical material. In this way, the spatialisation of the work makes tangible the terms of travel and place which lie at the heart of the concept of diaspora.

G and B as Home and Away

There are a number of ways that the differentiation between local, diaspora and outsider groups is represented musically in *Tradition-Hybrid-Survival*. One example is the way that the harmony of the piece is based on a bitonal tension between key centres of G, representing "home," and B, representing "away." As previously mentioned, the local group remain

entirely within the G tonal centre, and the outsiders exist only in relation to B while the diaspora group move between these two places. The
movement of the piece as a whole reproduces a journey from a place
of "home" towards a place of "away" since the work begins in the tonal
centre of G and ends in the tonal centre of B.

Numerous threads connect notes G and B with constructions of "home"
and "away" respectively. The Guidonian hand – a medieval device for
singers which assigns each note to a position on the hand – positions G
at the tip of the thumb, thus constructing it as a nominal "starting point"
from which all other note values unfold (Berger, 2002: 78). Similarly, the
note G exists as an open string on violins, violas, cellos, double basses,
kamanchehs (Iranian spiked fiddle), tars and setars (both Iranian lutes),
meaning this pitch can denote a kind of home for a whole range of instru-
ments. In part for these reasons, G is a common tonal centre for music
in each of the twelve modal organisations referred to as *dastgah* within
Iranian classical music practice.[4] In contrast, B is a common tonal centre
only for works in the *dastgah* of *Dashti* and also occasionally in *Shur*,
while B *koron* (a microtonal flattening) exists as a tonal centre for works in
Segah only.[5] Moreover, there are no B open strings on any of the western
or Iranian instruments considered here. As a result, the construction of G
as "home" and B as "away" functions as more than mere metaphor.

The home-away binary between G and B not only represents a function of these pitches in themselves but also references their relationship
with each other. Indeed, B exists in a state of distance from G due to
the relationship between the partials in their respective harmonic series. The harmonic series (or overtone series) refers to the set of pitches
that resonate naturally whenever a fundamental pitch vibrates. That is
to say:

> [W]hen you play a C, what you are hearing is a collection of over-
> tones associated to this pitch and this is applicable to any sound you
> hear coming from an instrument or otherwise. It's a natural physical
> phenomenon. . . . Using an analogy, just as the colors of a rainbow
> combine to make white light, the related notes in a harmonic series
> combine to make what we hear as a single pitch.
>
> (www.beyondmusictheory.org/the-harmonic-series/,
> last accessed 2 April 2023)

The differing volume or resonance of each of these partials gives sound
its unique timbre or texture. For example, a trumpet sounds like it does
in part because the fundamental and first four partials are all very strong.
This contrasts with the flute, which has a distinct fundamental but much
weaker partials, and the clarinet, wherein only odd-numbered partials
can be discerned. Returning to the relationship between the note values

of G and B, we might consider how their respective sets of partials contain a semi-tone dissonance (the third partial in the G harmonic series is the note D while the fifth partial in the B harmonic series is the note D#), which reinforces a sense of fundamental distance between these pitches.

Further, the note values G and B are framed by a system of western classical harmony based on tension and release within which harmonic-mediant relationships have particular qualities and associations. The degrees of the diatonic scale in western classical music all have particular names which denote their harmonic/melodic relationships to each other. For example, in a C major scale, degrees would be labelled as follows: C – tonic, D – supertonic, E – mediant, F – subdominant, G – dominant, A – submediant, B – leading note. Therefore "harmonic-mediant relationships" refer to a harmonic shift from the tonic to the mediant (or first to third degree of the scale) or, in this case, G to B. As Rothstein notes in his discussion of Italian romantic opera, harmonic-mediant relationships could be conceived as being:

> motivated by exoticism, a desire to portray the Other, whether that Other resided at a distance of time (the neo-medieval French romance) or of space (Mozart's "Moorish land," Mendelssohn's Scotland) from the composer's here and now.
>
> (Rothstein, 2008: para 53)

Similarly, Heine (2018: 107) suggests that harmonic-mediant relationships in romantic era Italian opera can sometimes be seen as signifying "a dramatic shift" in the action. In film music similarly connected to this lineage, these same progressions can be seen as referring to "magic, mythology, the 'fantastic'" (Heine, 2018: 107). Therefore, harmonic-mediant relationships in certain circumstances have a history of implying change, movement and an unknown distant locality.

As previously mentioned, in *Tradition-Hybrid-Survival*, the local group remain entirely within the G tonal centre, the outsiders exist only in relation to B and the diaspora group move between these two places. Within this piece, the G tonal centre and its representation of home is fairly harmonically diverse, including the G harmonic series, G minor and G Phrygian scale (a minor mode characterised by a flattened second degree. In this context, the G Phrygian scale is G A-flat B-flat C D E-flat F). The B tonal centre and its representation of a vague "away" is more simplified and refer only to B minor/major. The piece starts very clearly in the "home" space of G, beginning with a gradually emerging perfect fifth on the tonic of G (see Figure 4.5) [00:00–01:00 in recording], which develops into a tutti (all players) chord outlining the G harmonic series (see Figure 4.6) [04:40–05:45]. After this, much of the harmony of the middle

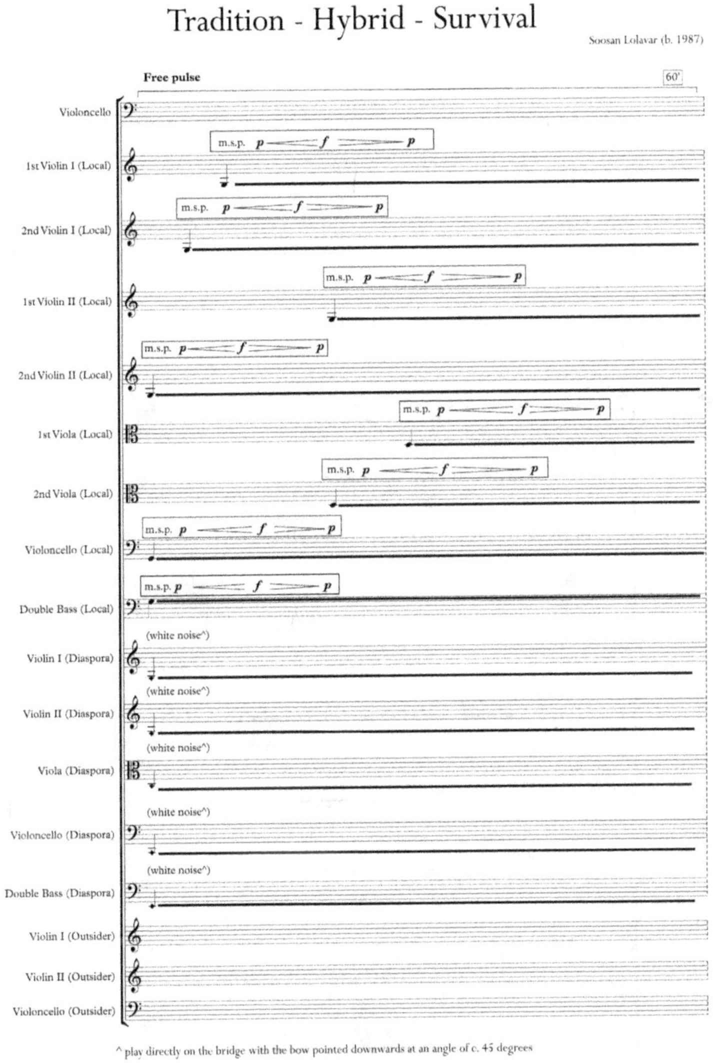

Tradition - Hybrid - Survival

Soosan Lolavar (b. 1987)

Figure 4.5 Opening of piece beginning with gradually emerging perfect fifth (G-D)

section of the piece is characterised by bitonality combining the tonal centres of G and B (see Figure 4.7) [07:25–07:45].

It is, perhaps, not especially surprising that a piece exploring ideas of "local" and "diaspora" experience would dramatically represent such ideas through musical representations of "home" and "away" and relate

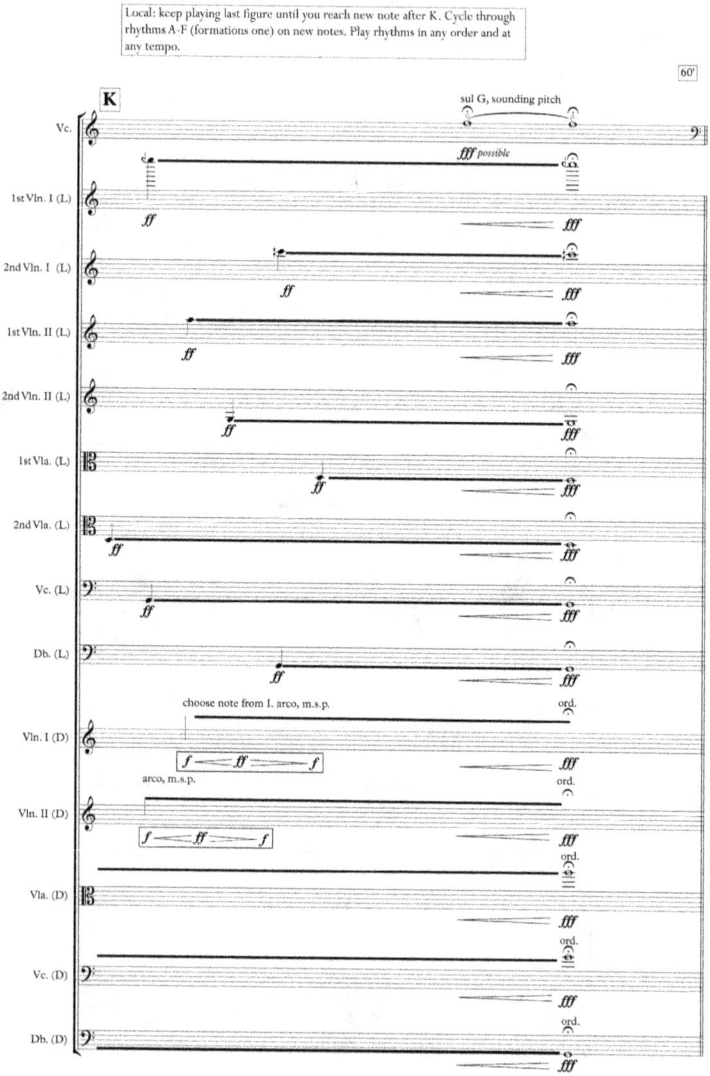

Figure 4.6 Chord depicting overtones of the harmonic series on fundamental G

these particular concepts to notes in the diatonic scale. What is important here is the ways in which understanding G and B as representations of "home" and "away" allows for a certain kind of embodied handling of these topics which has enabled me to understand Ingold's ideas of

Figure 4.7 Examples of bitonality between tonal centres of G and B. At letter O, "local" strings play a chord of G minor while "diaspora" strings play a chord of B major.

wayfaring and transport in new ways, and further how these embodied ways of knowing about wayfaring and transport relate to my own experience of diaspora. That is to say, my argument is not about the extent, value or meaning of these representations in my music, but rather about how seeing and exploring these representations through my music allows me to understand theoretical concepts in ways that might otherwise have remained invisible.

Composing as Embodied Knowing

At this point, it is pertinent to note that many of the previously described relations between identity groups and concepts of "home" and "away" emerged intuitively through the process of composing. Indeed, it was only *after* I had written this work, and during a period when I was reflecting on and analysing it, that I began to consider the meaning of these relationships. In the process of composing, I simply heard the opening of the piece as an unfolding chord based on the harmonic series. I chose the fundamental G partly for practical reasons because open strings on cellos, violas and violins would make this sound particularly resonant. Later, I developed the material for what at this stage I referred to as the "ripieno," the offstage group of musicians that would later become the outsiders. This idea for an unseen group of players was derived from my experience of a work by Edward Jessen called *Companion* (2008) in which this technique was used to great effect. I sat at the piano to write this material and played around with different ideas. What emerged from this process of handling was material in the tonal centre of B, specifically two chords which cycled back and forth (see Figure 4.8).

When creating this material for the ripieno, I aimed to create something which felt different from the material onstage, but the choice of a tonal centre with such a strong sense of implied distance from the centre of G (and concomitant implication of "home" and "away") was entirely intuitive. Or rather, this outcome was the result of deeply embodied ways of knowing derived from years of working with sound. I have been engaged in western classical music in some way since the age of six years old, and my explorations with the Iranian tradition began around 2011. While I did not explicitly aim to reproduce harmonic-mediant relationships or currents which denote G as "home" and B as "away" in both the western and Iranian classical traditions, it is likely that, on an embodied level, I understood such relationships and brought them to bear on my music.

Establishing key material for the piece in the tonal centres of G and B was an important early step in the process of bringing *Tradition-Hybrid-Survival* to life: once these materials took shape, a lot of the piece began to quickly unfold. In this way, these initial building blocks were much

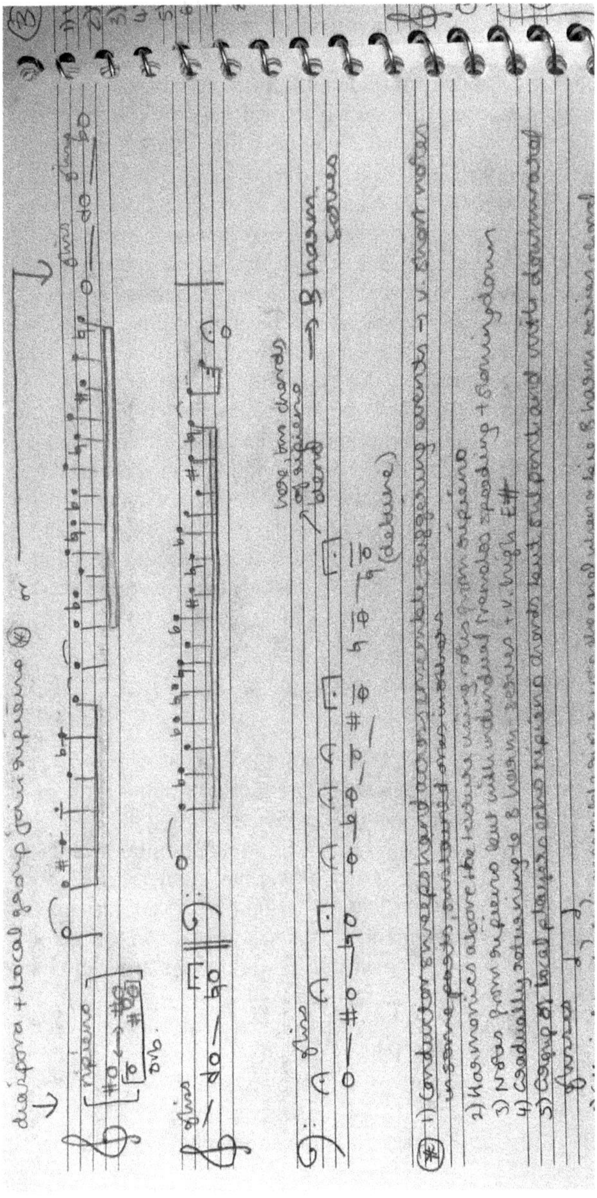

Figure 4.8 Early sketches of *Tradition-Hybrid-Survival* in which the material for the "ripieno" offstage group is developed in the tonal centre of B (first two chords of the system)

more than static objects. I, as the maker, did not simply consider and position these embryonic themes at will. Rather, G and B acted as vibrant and active materials with their own sense of movement and motion. I followed the flow of these materials to such an extent that I soon began to explore the technique of bitonality, crashing these tonal centres together to create a harmonic language characterised by instability and dissonance. In my early sketches for the work (see Figure 4.9), I wrote down this term, underlined twice for good measure.

At this stage, I had not yet considered that local players would remain in the G tonal centre and diaspora players would move between G and B. I had no conscious sense of bitonality dramatically representing the entangled concepts of "home" and "away" which is central to my experience of diaspora. Rather, I followed the flows of my materials to bring these ideas into being. This process took place against the backdrop of decades of life experience – explored throughout this book – in which the forces of diaspora have left an indelible mark on my life. Such experiences came into particularly sharp focus while composing this piece because, as I remarked in the programme note, I wrote it "during a period when I was travelling a great deal between the UK and Iran and had to constantly re-make myself as I moved between these very different places." I will consider the effects of this analysis on my understanding of theories of diaspora later, but at this point, it is interesting to note the ways that my experiences of double-consciousness are set in motion in certain elements of my music.

Tradition-Hybrid-Survival and Analogies of Wayfaring/Transport

Against the backdrop of tonal centres representing ideas of "home" and "away," I would argue that *Tradition-Hybrid-Survival* aligns with ideas of travel and place that were described previously in Ingold's model of transport. Specifically, despite brief moments which gesture towards the dynamism of wayfaring, the piece as a whole has a tendency to reproduce a notion of place as fixed, delineated and formed prior to any human (or non-human) entanglement. That is to say, place in this piece is not a function of our ongoing movement, but rather, it acts as an empty nexus which is then filled with human activity.

One of the key ways that this piece reproduces analogies of travel and place is through the particular kind of notation used to give directions to musicians. *Tradition-Hybrid-Survival* juxtaposes sections of traditional notation (see e.g. Figure 4.10) [11:56-12:30] containing clear directions in terms of pitch, rhythm, duration, volume and tempo, with more open sections (see e.g. Figure 4.11) [12:30-13:30] where musicians follow general text-based instructions in the score, allowing more freedom and flexibility. Focusing first on those instances of the piece which use less

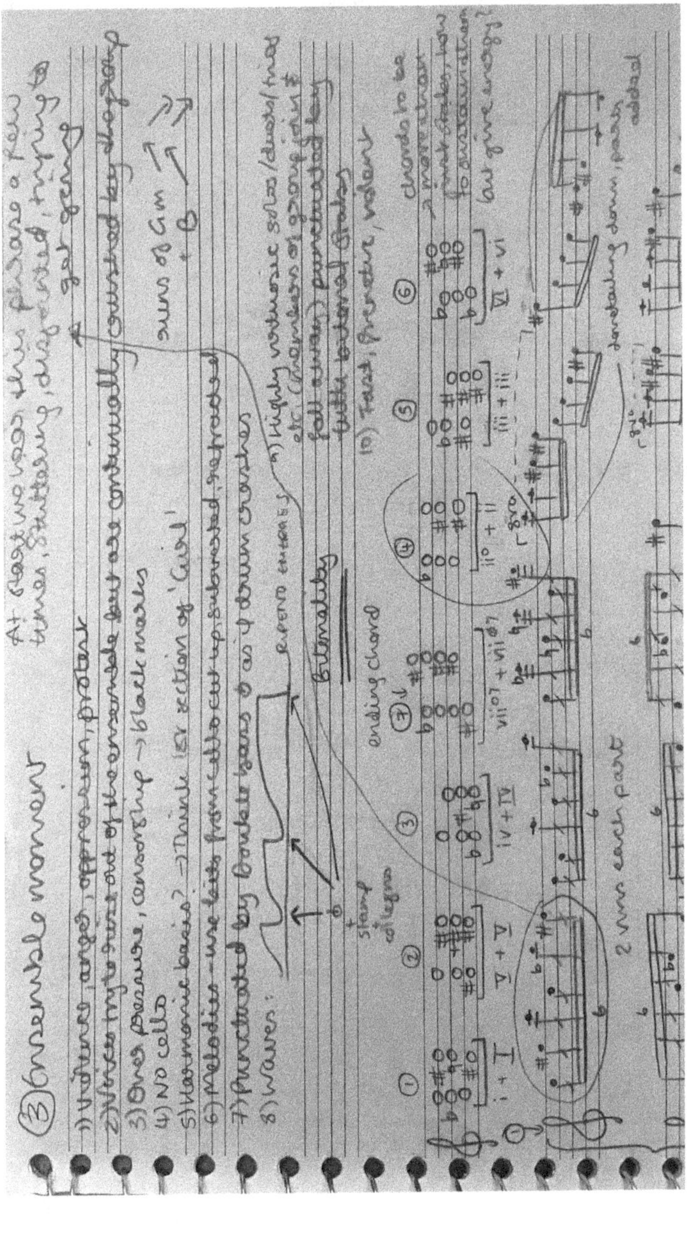

Figure 4.9 Early sketches of *Tradition-Hybrid-Survival*: the first mention of bitonality

Figure 4.10 A traditionally notated section of the score with clear directions in terms of pitch, rhythm, duration, volume and tempo

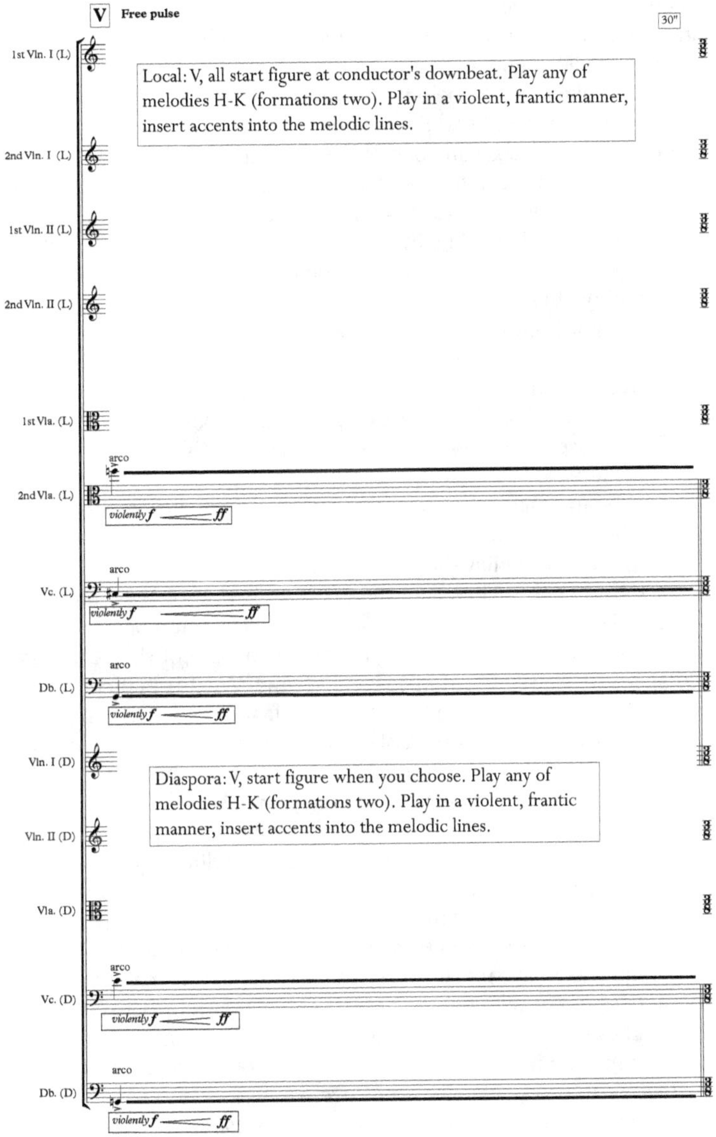
V
Free pulse
30"
1st Vln. I (L)
Local: V, all start figure at conductor's downbeat. Play any of melodies H-K (formations two). Play in a violent, frantic manner, insert accents into the melodic lines.
2nd Vln. I (L)
1st Vln. II (L)
2nd Vln. II (L)
1st Vla. (L)
arco
2nd Vla. (L)
violently f ff
arco
Vc. (L)
violently f ff
arco
Db. (L)
violently f ff
Vln. I (D)
Diaspora: V, start figure when you choose. Play any of melodies H-K (formations two). Play in a violent, frantic manner, insert accents into the melodic lines.
Vln. II (D)
Vla. (D)
arco
Vc. (D)
violently f ff
arco
Db. (D)
violently f ff

Figure 4.11 A non-traditionally notated section of the score where musicians follow general text-based instructions and have considerably more freedom and flexibility

conventional methods of notation, we might consider how they momentarily create a dynamism that is closer to the analogy of wayfaring.

For example, Figure 4.12 [12:30-13:30] shows how local players are directed to play a set of melodies, labelled H-K, which are depicted on an additional sheet entitled *Formations Two*. Directions in the score instruct players to choose any one of these melodies and play it at a chosen tempo beginning at the moment of the conductor's downbeat. This means that playing responds to centralised direction, after which point there is limited individuality. This results in an aural landscape where the local players have a moment of communion that gradually dissipates as they all follow their own tempo.

In this same section, we can observe how the diaspora group explores the same set of melodies as the local group but begins playing when they choose rather than following the conductor. This results in a blurred aural landscape in which both groups explore the same basic idea, but within which the diaspora players are more disjointed in this process than their local counterparts.

There is an analogy between the greater communion and directedness of the local players described here, and their status as persons of common cultural heritage who are co-present, and whose actions are directed into greater alignment through the sharing of laws, practices, codes and customs. Similarly, the diaspora players' sense of greater temporal dislocation echoes their positioning as people of shared cultural heritage who are separated in space and time. What is particularly relevant here is not the extent to which musical material represents the label of either local or diaspora place, but rather how the music enables the players to find their way *through* such material in a manner that brings local and diaspora place into being. That is to say, this short section of *Tradition-Hybrid-Survival* does not so much create local or diaspora space as a blank enclosure that is then filled with players, but rather it brings those places into being through creating the conditions for the players to move *along* such material in either a "local" or "diaspora" way.

Specifically, in the examples considered above, as well as various other moments in this piece, local and diaspora players make a series of decisions about how to enact and explore relationships between themselves. These choices include: selecting a melody from those labelled H-K and notated in Formations Two; deciding on a fast tempo at which to play this melody; selecting an octave within which to play; deciding how many times to repeat said melody; and choosing when to move to a different melody and make many of the same choices again.

The crucial difference here is that the local players all start this process at the same moment, while the diaspora players begin independently. This means that local players begin threading their way through this set of material with a sense of togetherness that gradually dissipates, while

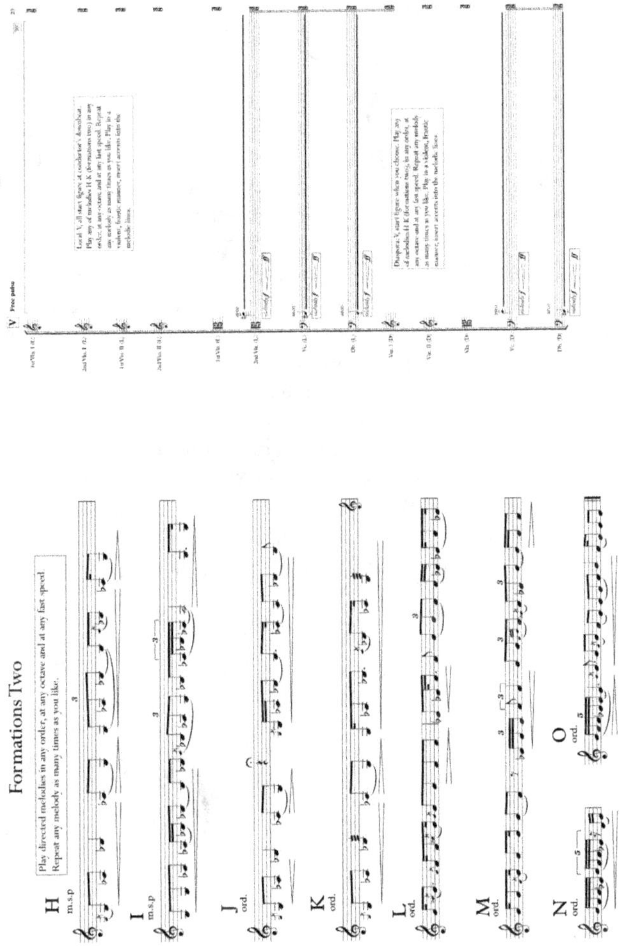

Figure 4.12 The local musicians play any of melodies H–K at their own speed, starting on the conductor's downbeat. Diaspora players explore the same idea but with a greater sense of freedom amongst themselves

diaspora players approach these instructions with a sense of individual-ism from the start. This subtle but important difference has the potential to affect the kinds of decisions players take in this section of the piece, evoking a way of moving *along* the musical material which is impacted by either a sense of relative togetherness or one of relative differentiation. These different ways of moving through the piece lay trails which also map onto our understanding of local-ness and diaspora-ness as places *brought into being* by the entanglement of such unfolding pathways.

Rather than considering place as an empty locus that is then filled with activity, Ingold's concept of wayfaring considers place as "like knots, and the threads from which they are tied are lines of wayfaring" (Ingold, 2008: 33). The sections of *Tradition-Hybrid-Survival* considered here fleetingly gesture towards a sense of local and diaspora place not as an enclosed field but rather as knots formed through the entanglement of a series of trails unfolded by players. These trails are dynamic. They respond to the lived moment-to-moment experiences of the instrumentalists and are broadly guided by (rather than enclosed by) general instructions in the score. Draw-ing on Ingold (2007; 2008), we might therefore consider how the move-ment *along* such musical pathways has the potential to bring the *places* of the local and the diaspora into being. This opens up a way of thinking through travel and place that aligns more with Ingold's model of wayfaring.

Despite these moments of wayfaring, the majority of *Tradition-Hybrid-Survival* reproduces the passivity of metaphors of transport. In order to further explore this, it is useful to consider Ingold's concept of the "logic of inversion" (see Figure 4.13) through which the pathways along which life is lived turn into the boundaries which enclose it (Ingold, 2008: 29). As he puts it, there is a tendency to "identify traces of the circumambulatory movements that bring a place into being as boundaries that demarcate

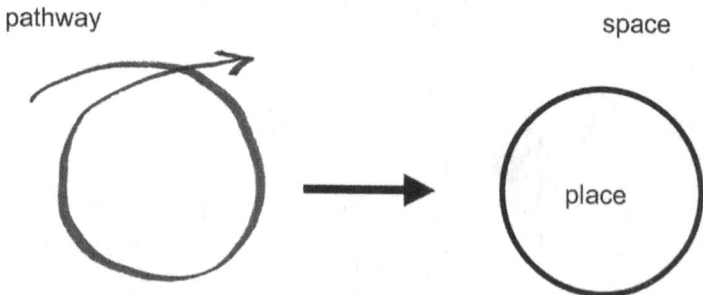

Figure 4.13 The logic of inversion transforming a pathway along which life is lived to a boundary which encloses it

Source: Ingold, 2008: 33

the place from its surrounding space" (Ingold, 2008: 32). This reproduces a notion of place as an empty locus which is then "filled" with activity.

As noted previously, Ingold asserts that lives are not enclosed by places but lived through, around, to and from them (Ingold, 2008: 33), and it is the ongoing living in these places that brings them into being as places "delineated by movement, not by the outer limits to movement" (Ingold, 2008: 34). In this way, the "logic of inversion" reproduces a notion of the world "that is occupied rather than inhabited, filled with existing things rather than woven from the strand of their coming into being in a world of space" (Ingold, 2008: 29).

The continuation of the above quote gives crucial further insight that is particularly relevant to my discussion of local and diaspora place:

> Indeed, it is for just this reason that I have chosen to refer to people who frequent places as "inhabitants" rather than "locals", for it would be quite wrong to suppose that such people are confined within a particular place, or that their experience is circumscribed by the restricted horizons of life lived only there.

It is pertinent that Ingold considers as "quite wrong" the term "locals," which is of such central importance to my exploration of travel and place within *Tradition-Hybrid-Survival*. Indeed, Ingold's very concerns – that the term "local" implies confinement and restriction – are borne out in my analysis of my piece. This is to say, many of the means of defining and delineating the local and diaspora groups in this piece have the effect of reproducing Ingold's logic of inversion, wherein both local and diaspora place are constructed as places which simply exist in the world. This overlooks the way that places are brought into being and instead reproduces metaphors of place and travel which are oriented towards transport.

A key way that transport-like ideas of travel and place are produced in *Tradition-Hybrid-Survival* is through the kinds of musical directions given in the more conventionally notated sections of the score. In those sections which give clear directions in terms of pitch, rhythm, duration, volume and tempo, the performers in the string ensemble can make very limited decisions about the sound they produce, and thus, their performing body as the *medium* of sound is rendered transparent and passive, instead of acting as a vessel for the composer's ideal vision. Here, the unfolding and dynamic reality of the performer-as-living-being is bracketed out in favour of a process by which they try to come close to a particular vision as detailed in the score.

Further, Ingold's model of wayfaring consistently emphasises the importance of bodily movement and, to a certain extent, the need for autonomy over that body in order to lay down a dynamic and winding trail. In contrast, *Tradition-Hybrid-Survival* features some sections which in their musical framing (and through many of the features of standardised western classical music practice) consciously limit the physical autonomy of the musicians involved and as such prevent them from engaging in the ongoing movement that characterises wayfaring. As a result, the fully notated sections of *Tradition-Hybrid-Survival* are likely to sound almost identical when performed by any ensemble in any location and time of year, day or night. Here, the bodies of the performers become incidental because of the ways in which they aspire to instantiate an ideal type of sound. In these sections, the experience of the musician comes close to reproducing the passivity of the passenger within a metaphor of transport.

Further, the functions of both the score and parts reproduce place as a defined locus within which players are *enclosed*. Individual instrumental parts provide each player with information limited to that particular group only. This separates the identity groups from each other such that a player who is labelled as "local" cannot unfold a trail which eventually intertwines with the knots of place marked as "diaspora," no matter the length of the journey they take. Equally, the physical placement of the performers on stage clearly demarcates the groups from each other – the local players are closest to the audience in a tight group, and the diaspora players are some distance behind, sat on a raised platform/stood in a single curved line. As such, both players and audience see local and diaspora groups as separate entities, or places within which players are *enclosed* and confined for the duration of the piece. Further markers such as the programme note (which refers to how the ensemble is divided into three groups), and the labelling of instrumental parts as "local," "diaspora" and "outsider," reproduce these groups as enclosed and delineated places.

To reiterate, in Ingold's analogy of wayfaring (and in our experience of the world), travelling from a place of "home" to a place of "away" is a journey that will involve an ongoing process of movement between places that are necessarily connected in the world. We do not exist in a place of "home," exit the world for a period of time and then re-enter in a new place labelled as "away." Despite this, *Tradition-Hybrid-Survival* represents musically exactly this kind of analogy of travel. Indeed, in the piece, there is no unfolding connection between these places caused by the laying down of trails, since players simply "arrive" in either of these two places after a period of transport.

We can see an example of this kind of process in the material of the diaspora group which vacillates between the "home" key of G and the "away" key of B. The way that players move between these key centres and their associations with place creates an impression of the key centres of G and B as terminus points at which the disembodied passenger "re-enters" the world from which they have been periodically alienated.

Such a relationship can be observed at rehearsal letters G to I (see Figure 4.14) [03:50-04:40] where the diaspora group occupy the "away" tonality of B. Then at rehearsal letter J [04:40-05:10], the lower strings in this group suddenly shift to the "home" tonality of G without any sense of an experiential and unfolding pathway connecting these two places. They remain in this "home" location until one bar before rehearsal letter O (see Figure 4.7) [07:20-07:45] when they are transported back to the "away" of a B tonal centre again. Because of the particular way that musical material is directed in the conventionally notated sections of *Tradition-Hybrid-Survival*, the locations of "home" and "away" exist as nodes on a route map, rather than as knots of activity formed out of the entanglement of unwinding trails of human existence. Indeed, place in *Tradition-Hybrid-Survival* simply *is*. This particular construction of place reproduces travel as a line which moves directly between specific nodes and destinations, and during which time the body of the traveller is exiled as it passively moves from pre-existing place to place.

A Wayfaring Coda

An important section of the piece which produces a very different way of thinking through travel and place is the extended coda, which takes place in the closing eight minutes of the piece. Here, the offstage outsiders play two pulsating chords in the "away" tonality of B as an accompaniment to an extended cello solo [15:35–end]. The outsiders play offstage and thus unconducted. The only tempo marking given in their part at this point is the vague direction "very slow." After several minutes, the rest of the ensemble are given instructions contained in Formations Three (see Figure 4.15) to *endeavour* to play along with the outsiders' refrain [18:20–end]. Due to the fact that the outsiders' part is very slow and unconducted, consists only of sustained notes, does not follow a clear rhythmic pattern and is played by unseen musicians, it is practically quite difficult for the local and diaspora players to correctly align their parts. Equally, while the outsiders play every note arco, the local and diaspora players are given a variety of techniques by which they can play any of the given notes. As a result, the local and diaspora players have to listen intently and play very sporadically and softly in order to align their playing with the outsiders' constant refrain.

A number of important actions are effected in this section of the piece. First, the outsiders choose a (very slow) tempo at which to play their refrain. Due to their aforementioned status as an offstage group, this tempo must be communicated amongst the three players through bodily movement only. Next, the rest of the ensemble must listen intently to this part to try to align their playing with one particular note from each of the two chords played by the outsiders. The ease with which an individual

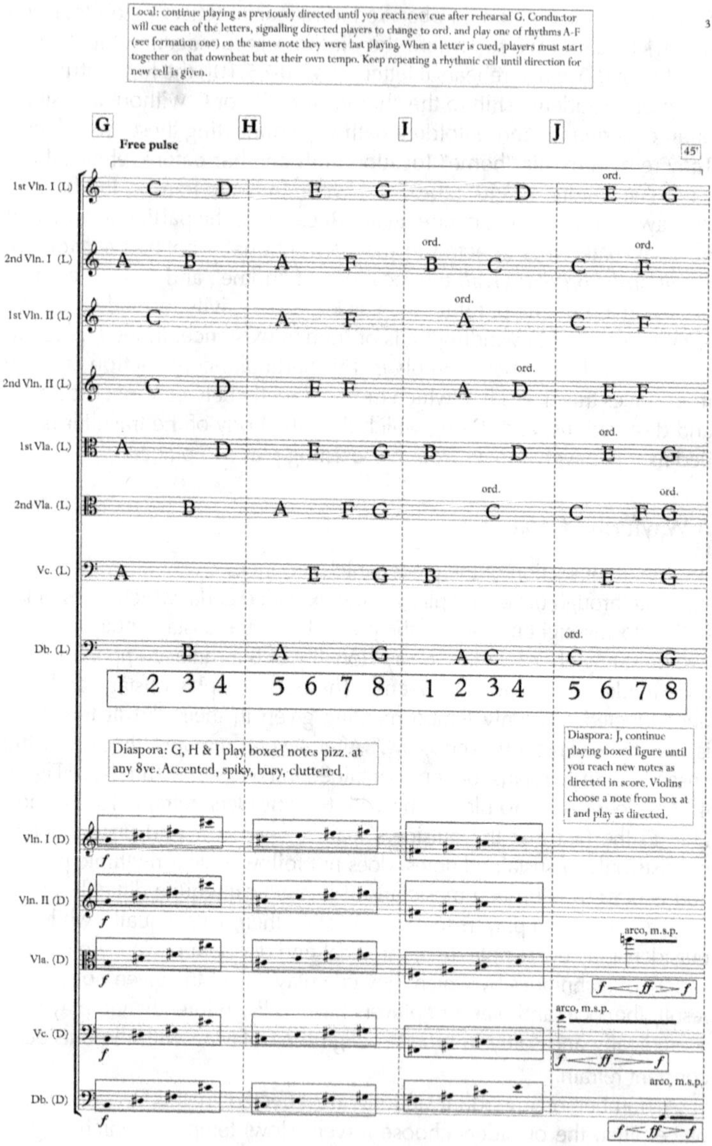

Figure 4.14 At rehearsal letter G, the diaspora group occupy the "away" tonality of B. Then at rehearsal letter J, the lower strings suddenly shift to the "home" tonality of G

Formations Three

> i. Play any pitches from these two chords (at any 8ve) following the directions in boxes P–U. Boxes can be repeated as many times as you like and played at any tempo. Listen carefully to the outsiders to ascertain the rhythmic movement between the two chords and try to play notes from the same chord being played by this group.

P

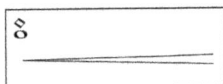

Q

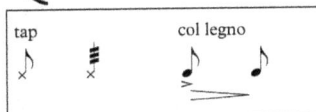

R

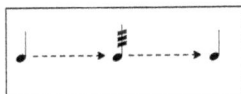

S

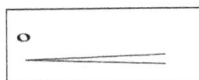

T

U

> ii. Continue to follow directions in i, but play a note from one of the two chords at any time, regardless of what chord may be occurring in the outsiders. This should produce the effect of the two chords merging and overlapping.

Figure 4.15 Instructions to diaspora and local players directing them to endeavour to play along with outsiders' refrain

can hear the outsiders' part and effect this alignment depends on where they are sitting onstage, the volume at which players around them are playing, their own hearing ability and the volume at which the outsiders are playing. Next, diaspora and local players have to choose one of the techniques (labelled P–U in Formations Three) by which to play a particular note from the outsiders' chords. Then, they must decide how many times to repeat this particular technique before changing.

As a result of these directions, all the players in the ensemble make a number of decisions which greatly affect the sonic outcomes of the piece. In this way, members of the string ensemble experientially pass *along* the world of the piece, reacting and responding to the sonic environment in which they are entangled. They unfold trails which have the dynamism and reactivity of Paul Klee's wayfaring "line that goes for a walk" and which stand in opposition to a straight line of transport connecting pre-conceived points. The body of the performer is no longer bracketed out or rendered transparent but instead becomes opaque and thick since it is their capacity to react to other performers – through visual and aural cues – that forms the basis of the sound they create. This section of the piece is concomitantly most reactive to time, space and the particular lived realities of the people who perform it since it will never sound the same twice. Moreover, the sense of place which is produced in this section of the piece is less dependent on a notion of delineated and a priori spaces which are then filled with humans and non-humans. Instead, place is *produced* through the entanglement of trails along which the ensemble pass. The dense, overlapping sound world in this section reproduces a notion of place as a series of knots formed from the entanglement of varied and complex trails. Here the members of the ensemble act as inhabitants playing an active and unfolding role in the creation of paths which then become intertwined in complex meshworks of place. In this way, the coda more fully realises the metaphor of wayfaring that is gestured towards in other parts of the piece.

In summary, *Tradition-Hybrid-Survival* explores notions of travel and place which align with Ingold's terminology of wayfaring and transport. While limited sections of musical material gesture towards a model of wayfaring – producing a dynamic and unfolding atmosphere in which musicians lay down pathways and trails – significant aspects of the piece reproduce the disembodied, point-to-point movement of transport and concomitant construction of place as fixed and delineated (Figure 4.16).

The implications of this analysis for our theoretical conception of diaspora will be explored in more detail below. In any case, and as noted previously, the extent to which *Tradition-Hybrid-Survival* can be proven to reproduce transport- or wayfaring-like ideas of place and travel is not the point of my analysis. Rather my aim in analysing my piece in this way is to produce a model for physically handling these metaphors that allows me to reflect on my life experience in new ways. As I will explain later, this experience of working with my music has encouraged me to see my understanding of my identity as deeply entangled with metaphors of transport. I believe this insight would have remained fundamentally unknowable without the capacity to handle such ideas in my music.

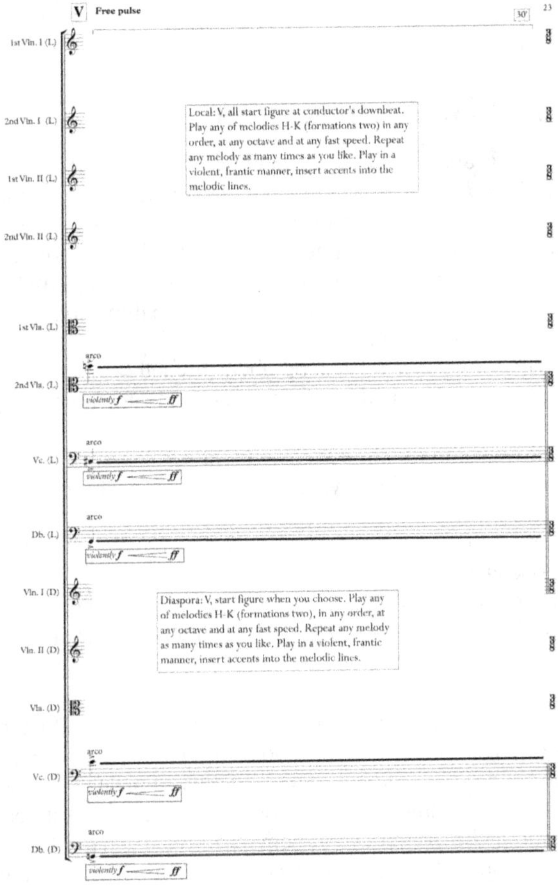

Figure 4.16 Example of greater independence amongst diaspora musicians

Furthermore, and as mentioned previously, it is pertinent to note that many of the musical decisions described were made intuitively during a period in my life when I was experiencing a great deal of the splittings of double-consciousness due to a period of intense travel. I think it is more than mere coincidence that I reproduced metaphors of transport which are characterised by alienation and separation from the embodied self at a time when I felt an intense sense of psychic splitting, and in a piece that was specifically focused on exploring local and diaspora identities. The benefit of an embodied approach entangling music composition and evocative life-writing is that I was able to see, hear and physically consider these relationships in my work and then use them to reflect on my life experiences.

Diaspora as Transport-Oriented Travel

The preceding analysis of constructions of place and travel within *Tradition-Hybrid-Survival* is intimately intertwined with a particular period of personal reflection on myself, my father and the ways that diaspora can be used as a frame to discuss our life experiences. Specifically, this framing came into focus due to my being struck by how regularly I make use of metaphors of transport to think about place and movement in my own life.

My entire vernacular for talking about my father's diasporic movement has, to this point, made use of transport-oriented terminology:

> My dad was born in Iran but came to the UK when he was 15 years old and then eventually stayed.

This oft-repeated refrain constructs my father as a passive and transported passenger between two fixed points, with the implication that he was static, motionless and "in place" at all times. When I try to think beyond such representations of him, other means of talking about my father emerge:

> While he was studying – first at a boarding school in Buxton in the north of England and then at school in London, during which time he lived in a series of south London bedsits – my father would return to Iran every summer. He made his way across the polluted streets of Tehran as he visited every member of his extended family, often extending up to the cooler north coast when the Tehran summer heat became too much to bear. As a young adult who could not afford the expensive plane ticket, he even drove to Iran with three friends, a trip which took them through Belgium, Germany, Austria, Yugoslavia, Bulgaria and Turkey and which they managed in five and a half days by sharing driving responsibilities and not stopping anywhere en route. He was in Iran during the Iran-Iraq war when Iraqi forces bombed the Tehran airport just before he was about to leave (he saw the Phantoms flying overhead), forcing him to spend 48 hours on a bus which travelled north through Iran and then west into Turkey and on to Istanbul. In fact, for the first 20 or so years of my life, my father would spend around three months in Iran every year, moving between his office, various family dwellings and the convention centre where the Tehran international book fair was held annually and at which he sold books.

And yet, my narratives about him still tend to focus on the delineated places of Iran and the UK as the so-called "poles" of his diasporic subjectivity. It is important to remember, therefore, that my father's migration was not a one-time event connecting two singular places but, rather, a series of trails which reached in various directions.

> When the Tehran airport was bombed, he was not trying to return to the UK but was rather making his way to Taiwan, which he eventually reached via Karachi and Bangkok. There's also the stories of when he and my mother took the Trans-Siberian railway from Moscow to Beijing, or when they travelled to Iceland to see the Northern Lights – my father's lifelong dream – and he was so upset that they didn't appear that he refused to get out of bed all day.

In any case, the stories offered here still tend to reproduce travel as international movement and my father as a traveller who skimmed the surface of the world, passively transferred from one enclosed place to another. The language of travel – especially when it comes to the kinds of large-scale international movement which characterise the diaspora frame – slips constantly into the language of transport, and the effects of this are significant.

Throughout my life, I understood Iran and the UK (the poles of my diasporic experience) as fixed and complete places which were separate from my and my father's lived experiences. The "home" and "away" of diaspora were places that *existed in the world*, between which our bi-cultural family was passively transported. I had no sense whatsoever of myself, my father or any member of my immediate family bringing the places of our diasporic experience into existence through our moving along the world. Our lives were fundamentally *enclosed* in places which existed as a priori loci of human and non-human activity. Such considerations of travel and place took on particular importance during a period in my life when the relationship between my father and me was particularly strained.

Diaspora, My Father and Me

From the time that I was about 10 years old, my relationship with my father would vacillate between explosive shouting and total non-engagement. Following the latest fight, my father would refuse to speak to me or even acknowledge my presence for days at a time, a situation which would make me so agitated that I would purposefully upset him again just to have him recognise that I existed. Sometimes it wasn't even anything I said. He was sensitive to any kind of loud noise, and I was constantly dropping plates and cutlery – partly because I was very clumsy but also because I knew it would annoy him. After each new *crash*, I would brace myself for the inevitable wave of fury to come my way. We argued constantly and incessantly. In many ways, it was a single argument which stretched on for 20 or so years.

Over the years, I've asked myself time and again what really caused all that pain and difficulty. If I were to excavate the reasons, I would admit that when I was very young, I hated having a foreign father. I remember asking my mother on several occasions if we could leave him and start a new family on our own. I used to dream of being more like the white children at my primary school – my fantasy was to have a dad who watched football and drank beer. When my father shouted at the television, it was to decry American imperialism or the evils of the west. He was strange and confusing, and I didn't like the way he drew attention to us as "not a normal family." I think, in a way, he always knew that; I can only imagine what it feels like to know that your child is trying to sabotage you. Looking back, I grew up with a deeply embedded prejudice against Iranians from a very young age. I *knew* that "those people" were not entirely trustworthy. At the same time, I never doubted that I was Iranian, too, and so gradually wove my own image into a tapestry tightly knotted with self-hatred. Here again, double-consciousness raises its head.

In part these feelings were unwittingly encouraged by my British mother. She has been married to my father for over 40 years and has loved and supported him throughout that time, but she had some confusing, difficult and humiliating experiences in Iran at the start of their relationship and has never really been able to get over them, in large part because her own complex childhood left her ill-equipped to address and process difficult emotions. It is partly due to these experiences that my parents returned to the UK, and I was born in London. I often think about this time as a pivot point precluding an alternative future in which my passport reads "born in Tehran," and my lifetime of wayfaring is no doubt severely attenuated. In any case, my mother's deeply buried hurt hardened, over many years, into a subtle, unacknowledged prejudice wherein many of the Iranian people she liked were described as "not like most Iranians." I absorbed this as a child and used it to justify a construction of my father as inherently problematic, a justification which, of course, reflected back on me in complex ways.

At the same time, my father was constantly disappointed that I behaved in ways that stood outside the norms of an Iranian childhood. He struggled to understand my Britishness and balked at the ways I was so entangled with a country that he still referred to as the "little Satan." When he was still living in Iran, he was nicknamed *taraghe* or "firecracker" because of his explosive and fiery temper. I believe now that every time he shouted at me, he was really expressing his anger, frustration and sadness at living so far away from his extended family.

From a young age, I understood all the ways in which my father and I failed to get along as entangled in the dynamics of diaspora. I wasn't Iranian enough for him, which made him angry and frustrated, and this anger and frustration was, for me, a representation of Iranianness which I experienced as confrontational and difficult. This funnelled all conflict in our family through the framework of the single and ultimate paradox between the fixed destinations of Iran and the UK and forced my father and me into the positions of occupying distinct, differentiated and ultimately opposing destinations. Such a construction left me with no means of conceiving of my own Iranian identity (how could I also be Iranian if to be so was to be like *him*?), so I left this part of me blank and unfulfilled.

But, of course, this whole characterisation of my father and me as occupying opposite ends of a diasporic binary is entirely false. On a very basic level, we are not merely respective representations of Iranian/ Britishness since I have always had a very strong sense of myself as an Iranian woman, and he has been a citizen of the UK for nearly 40 years. Further, we are – of course – intimately entangled in complex relationships of culture and family ties that knit together our lives and cannot simply be conceived under broad, national labels. My argument is that the tendency in my life to understand conflict through this binary paradigm is connected to the prevalence of transport as an analogy for thinking about place and travel and the particular ways this impacted my experience of diaspora.

Transport leaves no space for the unfolding and dynamic process of passing along the world, laying pathways which trail in multiple directions and become entangled in various knots of activity. While wayfaring constructs the traveller as consistently emplaced, transport alienates the traveller from the process of travel and considers them "in place" only when they have reached the fixed terminus of their destination or point of re-entry into the world. Thus, while wayfaring makes space for the traveller to be *some*where, which is always on its way to and from someplace else, transport considers the traveller as located in only one fixed and delineated location at a time. In short, the transport framework produces an analogy of my own diasporic experiences in which I am enclosed *either* in a place which is labelled as standing for Iranianness *or* in a place similarly labelled as British. Since the process of travel that links these two places is one in which the passenger is alienated and steps out of the world, there is no sense in which I can draw from or be connected to these two places at the same time through an experiential journey between them.

As has been discussed previously, Hall (1990), Clifford (1994) and Gilroy (1993) consider the diaspora frame to offer a way of thinking through identity – and its connection to concepts such as travel and place – that is dynamic and untethered to singular nation-states. It could be argued, further, that this model has emancipatory potential, both in the face of ethno-nationalist claims to purity and belonging and the psychological fragmentations of double-consciousness.

And yet, this potential of the framework of diaspora is blunted when it is based on a notion of travel and place which is encapsulated by the metaphor of transport. This is because the traveller is offered a model of diaspora in which they are enclosed in a place that is delineated, and from which the journey to another similarly defined place is characterised by alienation. This splitting of the self into defined places finds its corollary in the psychological fragmentation of double-consciousness. A transport-oriented notion of diaspora thus fundamentally lacks the means for theorising either how places are intimately connected and entangled, or how the traveller's position within this meshwork is one in which they are connected to multiple places at the same time.

My experiences of a transport-oriented notion of diaspora have caused me to perceive Iranianness as a defined and delineated place that exists in a full and complete sense outside my involvement with it. Iranianness was always a destination in which I was enclosed or a fixed place at which I could only arrive or depart. A notion of diaspora which constructs place and travel in transport-like terms causes me to experience the "here-there" of my diasporic binary as enclosing places which exist in a complete form outside my entanglement with them. Iranianness is thus constituted as defined, a thing or place from which the perceiver is alienated, and double-consciousness as an internalised form of subject-object dualism is triggered. In order to find a way out of this construction and realise the emancipatory potential of the diaspora paradigm we have to, I argue, turn to a notion of place and travel that is based on wayfaring – the driving force behind my composition *I Am the Spring, You Are the Earth*.

Wayfaring and *Ductus*

To outline the fundamentals of wayfaring as they operate within *I Am the Spring, You Are the Earth*, we might consider an analogy between wayfaring and particular kinds of reading and writing as discussed by Ingold (2007) in his work *Lines*. As he describes it, early-modern/modern ideas of writing and reading tend to produce transport-like notions of place and travel. That is to say, the writer is constructed as "a master of all he surveys, [confronting] the blank surface of a sheet of paper as much as the colonial conqueror confronts the surface of the earth" (Ingold, 2007: 13). In this construction, the text is an artefact that is brought into being on the previously blank space of the page. It is an object constructed by the writer, who acts as a cartographer, overseeing a wide and empty expanse on which they plot a course "even before setting out" (Ingold, 2007: 15). In this way, early-modern and modern notions of reading align with a process of navigation in which the reader passes through a series of pre-defined points in the text.

In contrast, thinkers from antiquity to the Middle Ages considered writing not as something that is made but as something which speaks to the reader with the voices of the past. Inscriptions have the quality of oral pronouncements, and the reader experiences them as such because of the ways they remember hearing texts spoken or sung out loud in their life. Reading is, therefore, not just a process of hearing but also a process of remembering previous experiences of hearing (Ingold, 2007: 14ff).

On this basis, if reading is a process of remembering, then writing is a process by which memory is inscribed. Writers from the Middle Ages considered the writer inscribing the surface of the paper as analogous to memory inscribing the surface of the mind (Ingold, 2007: 16). Crucially, these surfaces were not to be surveyed from afar (much like the navigator surveys a mapped landscape) but, rather, "through the laborious process of moving around" (ibid.). Consequently, a whole range of thinkers in this period referred to reading as a process of recollecting or gathering (Ingold, 2007: 15) much like hunting or fishing (Carruthers, 1990: 30; 247). As Leroi-Gourhan puts it, "[E]ach piece of writing was a compact sequence . . . around which the readers found their way like primitive hunters – by following a trail rather than by studying a plan" (Leroi-Gourhan, 1993: 261).

Thus, readers and writers in the period from antiquity to the Middle Ages moved through texts as wayfarers who, as Ingold puts it,

> did not interpret the writing on the page as the specifications of a plot already composed and complete in itself, but rather . . . as a set of signposts, direction markers or stepping stones that enabled them to find their way about within the landscape of memory.
>
> (Ingold, 2007: 16)

Medieval readers referred to this sense of flow guiding the reader from place to place as *ductus*, which Mary Carruthers describes as "the concept that an artistic work is a journey . . . the way by which a work leads someone through itself" (Carruthers, 2013: 190).

Central to the definition of *ductus* is a kind of travel which echoes the unfolding, flow-like nature of wayfaring as a means of passing through the world. It "insists upon movement, the *conduct* of a thinking mind on its *way* through a composition" (ibid., emphasis in original); it "flows along, like water in an aqueduct, through whatever kinds of construction it encounters on its way" (Carruthers, 1998: 78). Every work within which *ductus* operates "needs to be experienced as a journey, in and through whose paths one must constantly *move*" (ibid.: 81). It is particularly drawing on the concept of *ductus* that we might consider how *I Am the Spring, You Are the Earth* produces a sense of travel and place that aligns with the framework of wayfaring, and a key way this is evidenced is through the sense of experiential and unfolding flow that permeates the work.

I Am the Spring, You Are the Earth

I will now turn to a consideration of *I Am the Spring, You Are the Earth*. Drawing on a notion of *ductus* as "the way by which a work leads someone through itself" (Carruthers, 2013: 190), the formatting of this chapter encourages the reader/listener to experience both the music of *I Am the Spring, You Are the Earth* and this text-based discussion of it as an unfolding journey which echoes the flow-like nature of wayfaring (Figure 4.17). Consequently, this chapter is meant to be read while listening to a recording of the piece. Time stamps in the text connect a particular section of text with a certain section in the piece and are intended to guide the reader through the process. I now invite the reader to listen to a recording of *I Am the Spring, You Are the Earth* which can be found on the 2019 album *Stepping Back, Jumping In* by Laura Jurd and released on Edition Records. Then, turn to the next page to experience a wayfaring discussion of this work.

I Am The Spring, You Are The Earth

من بهارم تو زمین

Soosan Lolavar

2019

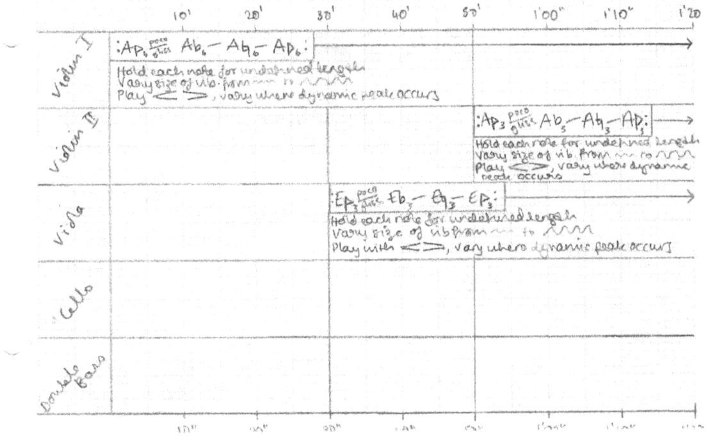

Figure 4.17 The opening bars of *I am the Spring, You are the Earth*.

[00:00]

The piece opens with a single violin note.

. . . [00:15] turn the page

[00:15]

This note expands into a 4-note figure, gently gliding between A *koron* (a microtonal flattening) – A-flat – A-natural – A *koron*.

. . . [00:30] Viola enters.

[00:30]

Viola enters and explores the same pattern of four notes starting on an
   E *koron*.

... [00:50] Violin II enters.

[00:50]

Violin II explores A *koron* – A-flat – A-natural – A *koron* at a lower octave.

The score for this piece eschews traditional five-stave notation and instead presents a series of graphically spaced, text-based instructions which leave considerable room for the players to make decisions about the precise sounds they produce. Each string player is assigned a particular octave within which to explore these pitches and a time stamp for when to begin playing.

. . . [01:20] Cello enters.

[01:20]

Cello imperceptibly enters.

Players are further guided to play these four notes with an undefined cre-
scendo/decrescendo expressive marking and also to employ vibrato as they
wish. Beyond these directions, the player must choose the duration of all
of the pitches they play, the degree and location of the crescendo/decre-
scendo, the particular dynamics they employ, and the range of vibrato they
will use.

. . . [01:40] Double bass joins.

[01:40]

Double bass joins the group.

Through the process of rehearsing and performing this piece, it became clear that the string players made dynamic decisions in all these areas on the basis of the sonic environment unfolding at that time.

. . . [02:30] Santoor solo.

[02:30]

Santoor solo begins.

The way players explored the more open aspects of the piece was never quite the same since it was dependent on the experiential moment in which such a trail unfolded. This emergent nature underscores the piece as a whole, producing an environment where instrumentalists experientially pass *along* the world of the piece, reacting and responding to the sonic environment in which they are entangled.

. . . [03:00]

[03:00]

The players are given no specific information as to the form their solos should take, and in practice, players tended to respond heavily to the sonic environment produced at that moment.

. . . [03:20] Guitar enters.

[03:20]

Guitar solo begins.

This piece has a *ductus*-like flow which is constantly moving and changing, since every utterance is connected to all other sounds which precede and follow it. Players reproduce a wayfarer-oriented mode of travel wherein they unfold trails along which each *somewhere* is always on its way to (and from) somewhere else.

. . . [04:15] Piano enters.

[04:15]

Piano solo begins.

The entanglement of these meshworks is such that the piece cannot really be cut or divided in a way that retains a clear sense of what it is, since every moment in the piece both unfolds out of something that preceded it and leads on to a moment that comes later.

As such, the piece is based on a number of experiential trails which are not fixed and delineated but rather reactive and unfolding.

. . . [05:20] Crescendo to brass entry.

[05:20]

Brass enters.

. . . [07:00] Gradual decrescendo.

[07:00]

Gradual decrescendo.

In any case, the recording of the piece presents only a single snapshot of its performance at that particular time and place. The piece continued to change and develop after it was captured in the form of a recording. The experiential pathway of the piece would later take in multiple performances, all of which contributed to the form the work took as it continued to grow and change.

. . . [07:40]

[07:40]

Fundamentally, there is no sense in which *I Am the Spring, You Are the Earth* actually exists as a final and complete work. It is a piece that is always in a state of becoming, iteratively produced in each new playing and listening.

This echoes a wayfarer-oriented mode of travel in which the traveller explores pathways which experientially unfold, as well as linking to the medieval concept of *ductus* as a means of passing through a composition like water flows through an aqueduct.

. . . [08:00] Electronics solo.

[08:00]

Electronics solo.

While this kind of travel was hinted at in some sections of *Tradition-Hybrid-Survival*, *I Am the Spring, You Are the Earth* unfolds entirely on this basis and therefore operates much more squarely within a framework of travel as wayfaring, rather than as transport.

. . . [08:45] End.

Diaspora as Wayfarer-Oriented Travel

I am struck by the relative ease with which I was able to paint the picture of my experiences of diaspora as transport-oriented travel and also by the difficulty I experience in perceiving the wayfaring-oriented version. In writing about diaspora-as-transport, I was able to draw on a huge well of life experiences and recount stories which I have perfected and honed over hundreds of retellings. I knew instinctively what the outcomes of such a conception of diaspora could be because I felt them deeply in my very being. I knew what it felt like to think of yourself as split in two, as existing in one place *or* another. I know what that fissure is because I felt it for a long time. But diaspora-as-wayfaring remains somewhat more elusive because it is a concept that has not guided my beliefs and ideas about my Iranianness. I can imagine that to experience diaspora as a form of wayfaring would allow me to feel intimately and simultaneously connected to the places of Iran and the UK. It would enable me to recognise that all the pathways I unfold are in some way connected to those two dense knots of place (as well as many others) as a result of their entanglement in the wider meshwork that is my life.

I can imagine conceiving that there is no sense in which defined and delineated places exist in the world and, thus, no sense of an "Iran" or "UK" outside my unfolding relationship with the poles of my diasporic experience. Indeed, a model of wayfaring might ultimately help me envisage my experiences of diaspora as a differential becoming in which I am intimately entangled, created moment to moment as I pass through the world. It might also help me understand the ways in which my father and I are entangled in a constantly growing and changing relationship that is not necessarily defined by antagonism and binary opposition and in which we are *both* trying to navigate complex relationships of place and travel. I can imagine that perceiving my diaspora self as a wayfarer might bring me curiosity and a sense of calm. I imagine all this because the thoughts detailed here describe a range of ongoing and complex experiential shifts in perception that unfold like a series of intertwined trails.

The point is that none of these new ways of thinking can be understood from a distance since they are not stops on a route map which can be checked off one by one. Rather, they are a series of entangled pathways which loop across, between and amongst one another, trailing off in other directions into areas of my life not touched on in this chapter. To really conceive of diaspora as a form of wayfaring is to experientially move along the paths unfurled as a result of this perceptual shift. Crucially, the form and shape of such pathways do not reveal themselves before you have set out, since a conception of diaspora-as-wayfaring is a path you follow, not a framework you look upon like a cartographer surveys a map. My first steps along this pathway seem to suggest a way of reconciling the fragmentations of double-consciousness, moving towards a new understanding of diaspora which lives up to its purported emancipatory potential.

Notes

1 *Inventory of My Life* is a 60-minute work for dancer, santoor performer, tape and projections which was performed in varying iterations in Cambridge (August 2018), Tokyo (September 2018) and London (May 2019). It was collaboratively produced by Kae Ishimoto – a Japanese performer working across Butoh and contemporary dance – Rosa van Hensbergen – a poet, maker, animateur and researcher on Japanese dance – and myself, inhabiting the role of santoor performer/composer.
2 https://www.facinghistory.org/standing-up-hatred-intolerance/warsan-shire-home
3 For further discussion of this piece, see also Lolavar (2022).
4 Derived from extensive conversations with Iranian classical musicians between 2019 and 2020, particularly the composer Davood Jafari.
5 ibid.

5 Entangled Pathways

Double-Consciousness and Diaspora

This project has used a triangular model of methods (enjoining analytical knowledge, practice-based ways of knowing through music composition and experiential knowledge expressed through evocative life-writing) to explore the extent to which the framework of diaspora can help reconcile the fragmentations of double-consciousness. This process brings nuance and detail to our understanding of the diaspora metaphor through a performative, embodied approach. At the same time, it has contributed to the growing discussion around practice-as-research in music, in particular the question of how to develop methodologies that allow for the broader dissemination of this kind of knowledge.

Against this backdrop, *Tradition-Hybrid-Survival* provides the setting for an exploration of the diaspora frame through the lens of Ingold's concepts of wayfaring and transport. By exploring the construction of place and travel within this composition, I develop a concept of transport-oriented diaspora as characterised by alienation and binary dualism. This frame reproduces an analogy of my own diasporic experiences in which I am enclosed *either* in a place which is labelled as standing for Iranianness *or* in a place similarly labelled as British. Since the process of travel that links these two places is one in which the passenger is alienated and steps out of the world, there is no sense in which I can draw from or be connected to these two places at the same time. Here, the diaspora frame fails to reconcile the fragmentation of double-consciousness and perhaps even reinscribes the binary dualism at its centre.

The composition *I Am the Spring, You Are the Earth* is next explored by way of a written text which echoes the *ductus*-like flow of the sound it describes. The words on the page gesture towards a kind of movement defined by ebb and flow, unveiling insight gradually as the reader traverses the narrative. In contrast to the fragmented texts of Chapter 3, which gesture towards the fragmentation of double-consciousness, the unfolding and open-ended quality of the text which describes and explores

DOI: 10.4324/9781003351450-5

I Am the Spring, You Are the Earth implies the very kind of dynamism that could point towards the reconciliation I seek.

This section points to a notion of diaspora infused with the concept of wayfaring. This new framing is crucially based on a notion of identity that is dynamic, syncretic, emergent and tied to multiple locations at once, a state echoed by the rhythm and cadences of the very text which describes it and the composition from which these insights derive. A conception of diaspora that is oriented towards wayfaring opens up a series of important pathways that relate to the experience of double-consciousness. Crucial amongst these is the way this particular framing enables a sense of intimate and *simultaneous* connection to the places of Iran and the UK. Rather than presenting these places as distinct enclosures, wayfaring highlights how all the pathways I unfold are in some way connected to those two dense knots of place (as well as many others) as a result of their entanglement in the wider meshwork that is my life. Thus, "Iran" and "UK" are conceived not as defined and delineated places that exist in the world but, rather, as knots of entanglement caused by my passing along the world. Fundamentally, this engenders a conception of my diasporic identity as continuously emergent. In this way, a wayfarer-oriented conception of diaspora has the potential to produce the emancipatory model of identity that Hall's (1990), Clifford's (1994) and Gilroy's (1993) framing of diaspora describe.

It is certainly the case, however, that in my attempts to move past the binary of coloniality in the diaspora frame, the politics that undergird the potential violence of migrancy have become somewhat obscured. Since the aim of my project is to explore the extent to which diaspora can contribute to a reconciliation of double-consciousness, and due to the fact that a wayfarer-oriented mode of diaspora has proved highly effective in my own experience, I argue for the efficacy of this model in this case. This specific, intimate focus on my own experiences has, however, shone a light on the continued need to consider experiences of diaspora as *unique* and *multitudinous*. Furthermore, it points to the ongoing tension within the emancipatory frame of diaspora: namely, that in offering a conception of identity as emergent and based on multi-locationality, there is an inherent danger of de-centring the uneven politics of migrancy.

Indeed, Avtar Brah has long called for self-reflexive, autobiographical accounts in discussions of diaspora, which she argues

> ought not to be theorised as transhistorical codifications of eternal migrations, or conceptualised as the embodiment of some transcendental diasporic consciousness. Rather, the concept of diaspora should be seen to refer to historically contingent "genealogies" in the Foucauldian sense of the word.
>
> (Brah, 1996: 192)

Genealogies of diaspora focus on specific lived experience and offer multi-layered and personal means for talking about migrancy, indigeneity, place, belonging, difference and commonality. Writing in 2010, Knott pointed out that authors had not yet fully examined the complexity of such experiences (Knott, 2010: 83). My highly personalised account answers this call.

New Methodologies

It is through the insights discussed here that I argue the case for an entangled methodology of music composition and evocative life-writing as adding important nuance to our understanding of diaspora. These methods of physical engagement with materials which highlight and excavate embodied forms of knowing have facilitated consideration of the psychic, emotional effects of diaspora, moving this term away from a detached, constative frame and towards the Foucauldian genealogies that Brah (1996: 192) mentions. That is to say, through deep analysis of my music, I was able to produce a model for physically handling metaphors of double-consciousness and diaspora which allowed me to reflect on my life experience in new ways. This project further aims to highlight the essentially performative nature of all knowledge-producing practices since there is no detached, transcendent observation of either double-consciousness or diaspora that stands outside our intimate physical engagement with the world from which these terms derive. Indeed, knowledge-producing practices are, in essence, materially engaged means of research *in the world* since the subject cannot step outside the world in order to analyse and observe it. This raises a number of important questions: namely, how much do we fail to grasp when we study the world in ways that overlook our essential experience of it? What more could we learn of theoretical concepts when we approach them through embodied methodologies which highlight and explore the fundamental bodily means through which we inhabit the world?

This book has also worked towards rendering tangible the complex process of arts practice in music. As I have explored, notated instrumental composition is often considered an elusive and slippery form of art practice which finds itself largely exiled from interdisciplinary discussion. Untangling this way of knowing involves translating into language a process that is not necessarily amenable to this means of representation. In this project, this has meant intertwining music composition with evocative life-writing, such that a text-based practice which similarly focuses on physical engagement with materials and embodied forms of knowing can bridge the linguistic gap between certain aspects of music composition and broader research communities. This practice is further developed through the use of non-standard textual formatting at various points in this book.

Through ordering and presenting texts in ways that differ from standard practice, I attempt to bring some sense of the embodied, unfolding relationship between listener and music, person and life experience, to the relation between reader and text. These ways of experiencing the world are, of course, distinct. The fact that music is an artform that unfolds in time is one of many reasons that the process of reading words on a page – words which can be stumbled over, repeated, skipped or skimmed at will – cannot be considered directly analogous. Despite this, the methods in this book explore ways of representing scholarly work that entangle the embodied ways of knowing defined by music composition and evocative life-writing with the means of representing that work through the written word. It is not enough for embodied work to be confined to one part of the scholarly process and exiled from another. If the "reflecting" and "analysing" portions of my practice are defined by practical engagement with materials, then a key focus of my future work will be to sustain this embodied engagement into the "representing" stage also. My practice in this area is still developing, and I look forward to discovering further means to approach text writing with the same energy I bring to music composition.

In this project, non-standard textual formatting is used, particularly in Chapter 3, and the final section of Chapter 5. In Chapter 3, discussions of double-consciousness and diaspora are disrupted by other styles of text writing which explore my personal relationship to these terms. Drawing on the work of Lau (2002), Moriarty (2013) and Turner (2013), I create a fragmentary, multi-layered text that moves continuously between analytical and embodied forms of knowledge. This disrupted style gestures towards my own experiences of these topics while highlighting some of the splittings of double-consciousness as I experience them. It also attempts to discourage passive reading since the reader has to constantly move backwards and forwards through the text, effecting a kind of correspondence through which meaning is ascertained. This chapter, therefore, at once offers a model of the splittings of double-consciousness *and* gestures towards the very kinds of embodied knowledge which are central to my exploration of these terms. In this way, this section outlines the fundamental shape of what is at stake in this book as a whole.

In contrast to the texts of Chapter 3, which represent the fragmentation of double-consciousness, the undulating, unfolding and open-ended quality of the text which describes and explores *I Am the Spring, You Are the Earth* gestures towards the very kind of dynamism that could point towards the reconciliation I seek. This means that it is not only the *content* of the text in this closing section but also the rhythmic flow of the text (itself entangled with a sense of movement found in a particular musical work) which points to a consideration of diaspora infused with the concept of wayfaring. This new framing is crucially based on a notion of identity that is dynamic and whose trails unfold in multiple directions, a state echoed by the rhythm and cadences of the very text which describes it and the composition from which these insights derive.

Double-Consciousness and Me

Central to this book has been an exploration of my experiences of double-consciousness, with a particular focus on how new ways of thinking about the frame of diaspora can facilitate a reconciliation of this internalised binary opposition. As a result, this project has involved a deep level of internal, psychic and emotional work. It is no exaggeration to say that my life has been fundamentally changed over the many years of working on this project. At the very least, my understanding of my father has transformed to such an extent that I now feel uneasy about some of the representations of our relationship in this book, written at an earlier time when everything was different.

While "reconciliation" has been discussed in this book, a question still remains around what this (internalised and subjective) process actually involves in detail and how, for that matter, one could even measure whether it has been achieved. In part, this ambiguity in the text is a rhetorical device, born out of the fact that I had no idea what reconciliation might mean when I set out on this project and wanted to recreate this feeling of gradual discovery for the reader also. Moreover, while the aim of reconciling double-consciousness has certainly been a key impetus and guiding principle of this project, it is really the process of walking a pathway in this direction – rather than the capacity to definitively reach this terminus or otherwise – that has emerged as most relevant in my work.

Even so, I am able to reflect on the way particular experiences over the last few years have helped alleviate some of my feelings of psychological fragmentation and, thus, draw a sketch of how I have experienced reconciliation in this time. This has largely involved a significant perceptual shift, enabling me to produce new frameworks of my identity which, in turn, help create a sense of distance between myself and the feelings of inadequacy that are engendered by double-consciousness. Until recently, I had spent a lifetime reproducing my identity as fragmented and incomplete. These beliefs – which I am now able to represent through a metaphor of transport-focused diaspora – were so central to my understanding of myself that I could not even conceive of them as perceptions; they simply felt like reality.

The processes engendered by this project have made space for an alternative perception of the "poles" of my diasporic subjectivity not as defined places between which I am passively transported but, rather, as dense knots of entanglement formed out of the trails laid by my very passing along the world. Such a shift in perception enables me to separate myself from the rising sense of panic I still experience when I feel unable to define and explain my identity. But crucially, I am now more able to understand these fears not as a *sign* of my inherent inadequacy but, rather, as a *symptom* of my complex and ongoing experiences.

A recent encounter exemplifies the effect of such processes in my daily life. In 2020 I was asked to take part in a series of events at a UK music festival focusing on music inspired by the work of Hafez, the 14th-century Iranian Sufi poet. I was asked to both speak on a panel discussing the contemporary influence of Hafez on music in Iran and introduce the evening's concert of Iranian and Kurdish music. These kinds of events are a not uncommon occurrence in my life and work, and, of course, there is nothing unusual about asking academics to speak publicly on areas connected to their research. Even so, I was left unsure if I would agree to such events in the future.

Due to the intense internal work that I have undertaken as part of this book, I have gradually become aware of the emotional weight of events like these, which produce me as some kind of "cultural bridge" (or, perhaps more accurately, where I feel compelled to produce *myself* as such). From a very young age, I believed it was my personal role to connect the poles of my hybridity through constant and ongoing processes of translation, and my continuing failure to achieve this left me feeling broken and unfulfilled. It has been remarked that "mixed race families are sometimes heralded as the ultimate antidote to racism, and a signifier of racial progress."[1] In my experience, however, bi-cultural family dynamics can effect a huge emotional cost on the children of such relationships. I always felt that the "emancipatory" meeting point between ideals of Iranianness and Britishness was located within my very existence and that if (and when) this failed to materialise, the fault was mine. I see these feelings now as a clear representation of my struggle with double-consciousness.

As a result of my experiences working on this project, a new understanding of myself has emerged in which I reject the notion of my identity as a mixture or bridge between fixed and bounded cultures. Instead, I find peace in the idea that my particular experiences of diaspora have created something else, something which is complexly related to ideas of Britishness and Iranianness (as well as many others) but which is fundamentally different from both. The gradual emergence of this way of thinking is clear in the chronology of the compositions presented as part of this submission. While *Tradition-Hybrid-Survival* (2017–8) engages in delineated and bounded ideas of Britishness/Iranianness or localness/diasporaness, *I Am the Spring, You Are the Earth* (2019) gestures towards a more individual sense of diaspora that is defined largely by itself, connected to the so-called poles of my hybrid identity but not defined by either, whether in isolation or in combination. While it is an ongoing project to truly shift the internal dialogue of a lifetime, the first steps along this unfolding trail are filled with hope and possibility.

Note

1 https://gal-dem.com/my-mum-calls-me-the-n-word-the-reality-of-growing-up-mixed-race-with-a-racist-parent/ (last accessed 13 February 2023).

Bibliography

Abu-Lughod, Lila. 1991. "Writing Against Culture." In *Recapturing Anthropology: Working in the Present,* edited by Richard G. Fox, 137–62. Sante Fe: School of American Research Press.

Adams, Jess, and Allan Owens. (Eds.) 2021. *Beyond Text: Learning through Arts-Based Research.* Bristol and Chicago: Intellect.

Ahmed, Sara. 2017. *Living a Feminist Life.* Durham, NC: Duke University Press.

Anderson, Leon. 2006. "Analytic Autoethnography." *Journal of Contemporary Ethnography* 35 (4): 373–95.

Ansari, Ali M. 2003. *Modern Iran since 1921: The Pahlavis and After.* Harlow: Pearson Education Limited.

Anzaldúa, Gloria. 2012. *Borderlands/La Frontera: The New Mestiza.* Fourth Edition. San Francisco, CA: Aunt Lute Books.

Austin, John L. 1975. *How to Do Things with Words: Second Edition (William James Lectures).* Cambridge, MA: Harvard University Press.

Back, Les and Nirmal Puwar. 2012. "A Manifesto for Live Methods: Provocations and Capacities." In *Live Methods,* edited by Les Back and Nirmal Puwar, 6–17. Oxford: Blackwell.

Bakan, Danny L. 2016. "'The Fountain Pen': Song and Storying through a/r/tographical Conversation with Senile Dementia." *Creative Approaches to Research* 9 (1): 4–18.

Barad, Karen Michelle. 2007. *Meeting the Universe Halfway : Quantum Physics and the Entanglement of Matter and Meaning.* Durham and London: Duke University Press.

Barrett, Estelle, and Barbara Bolt. (Eds.) 2010. *Practice as Research: Approaches to Creative Arts Enquiry.* London: I.B. Tauris.

———. (Eds.) 2013. *Carnal Knowledge: Towards a New Materialism Through the Arts.* London: I.B. Tauris.

———. (Eds.) 2014. *Material Inventions: Applying Creative Arts Research.* London: I.B. Tauris.

Bartleet, Brydie-Leigh, and Carolyn Ellis. (Eds.) 2009. *Music Autoethnographies: Making Autoethnography Sing/Making Music Personal.* Bowen Hills, Queensland: Australian Academic Press.

Berger, Karol. 2002. "The Guidonian Hand." In *The Medieval Craft of Memory,* edited by Mary Carruthers and Jan M. Ziolkowski. Philadelphia: University of Pennsylvania Press.

Bolt, Barbara. 2010. "The Magic Is in Handling." In *Practice as Research: Approaches to Creative Arts Enquiry*, edited by Barbara Bolt and Estelle Barrett, 27–34. London and New York: I.B. Tauris.

———. 2016. "Artistic Research: A Performative Paradigm." *Parse Journal* 3: 129–42.

Brah, Avtar. 1996. *Cartographies of Diaspora: Contesting Identities*. London: Routledge.

———. 1999. "The Scent of Memory: Strangers, Our Own, and Others." *Feminist Review* 61 (Snakes and Ladders: Reviewing Feminisms at Century's End, Spring): 4–26.

Brah, Avtar, and Annie E. Coombes. (Eds.) 2000. *Hybridity and Its Discontents: Politics, Science, Culture*. London: Routledge.

Bresler, Liora. 2005. "What Musicianship Can Teach Educational Research." *Music Education Research* 7 (2): 169–83.

Bull, Michael. 2000. *Sounding Out the City: Personal Stereos and the Management of Everyday Life*. Oxford: Berg.

Bulkin, Elly, Minnie Bruce Pratt, and Barbara Smith. 1984. *Yours in Struggle: Three Feminist Perspectives on Anti-Semitism and Racism*. New York: Long Haul Press.

Carruthers, Mary. 1990. *The Book of Memory: A Study of Memory in Medieval Culture*. Cambridge: Cambridge University Press.

———. 1998. *The Craft of Thought: Meditation, Rhetoric and the Making of Images, 400–1200*. Cambridge: Cambridge University Press.

———. 2013. *Rhetoric Beyond Words: Delight and Persuasion in the Arts of the Middle Ages*. Cambridge: Cambridge University Press.

Chanan, Michael. 1994. *Musica Practica*. London and New York: Verso.

Chang, Heewon. 2008. *Autoethnography as Method*. Walnut Creek, CA: Left Coast Press.

Chrisman, Laura. 1993. "Journeying to Death: Paul Gilroy's the Black Atlantic." In *Postcolonial Contraventions: Cultural Readings of Race, Imperialism, and Transnationalism*, 73–88. Manchester: Manchester University Press.

Ciccariello-Maher, George. 2009. "A Critique of Du Boisian Reason: Kanye West and the Fruitfulness of Double-Consciousness." *Journal of Black Studies* 39 (3): 371–401.

Cixous, Hélène. 1976. "The Laugh of the Medusa." Translated by K. Cohen and P. Cohen. *Signs*. Vol. 1: 875–93.

Clarke, Eric F. 2005. *Ways of Listening: An Ecological Approach to the Perception of Musical Meaning*. New York: OUP.

———. 2010. "Rhythm/body/motion: Tricky's contradictory dance music." In *Musical Rhythm in the Age of Digital Reproduction*, edited by Anna Danielson, 105–20. Farnham: Ashgate.

Clifford, James. 1994. "Diasporas." *Cultural Anthropology, Vol. 9, No. 3, Further Inflections: Toward Ethnographies of the Future (Aug., 1994)* 9 (3): 302–38.

———. 1997. *Routes: Travel and Translation in the Late Twentieth Century*. Cambridge, MA: Harvard University Press.

Clifford, James, and Vivek Dhareshwar. (Eds.) 1989. *Traveling Theories, Traveling Theorists*. Santa Cruz, CA: Group for the Critical Study of Colonial Discourse & the Center for Cultural Studies U.C.S.C.

Clifford, James, and George E. Marcus. (Eds.) 1986. *Writing Culture*. Berkeley: University of California Press.

Cole, William Davy. 2017. *Expanded Musical Form*. PhD Diss. City, University of London.

Croft, John. 2015. "Composition Is Not Research." *Tempo*, 69 (272): 6–11.

Culkin, J. 1967, March 18. "A Schoolman's Guide to Marshall McLuhan." *Saturday Review*, 51–3, 70–2.

Deleuze, Gilles and Félix Guattari. 2004. *A Thousand Plateaus: Capitalism and Schizophrenia*. Translated by B. Massumi. London: Continuum.

Denzin, Norman K. 2014. *Interpretative Autoethnography. Qualitative Research Methods*. Vol. 17. Thousand Oaks, CA., USA: SAGE Publications Ltd.

Derrida, Jacques. 1981. *Positions*. Translated by A. Bass. Chicago: University of Chicago Press.

Dirlik, Arif. 1994. "The Postcolonial Aura: Third World Criticism in the Age of Global Capitalism." *Critical Inquiry* 20 (2): 328–56.

Doğantan-Dack, Mine. 2015. *Artistic Practice as Research in Music: Theory, Criticism, Practice*. Farnham: Ashgate.

Drever, John Levack. 2002. "Soundscape Composition: The Convergence of Ethnography and Acousmatic Music." *Organised Sound* 7 (1) April: 21–7.

Du Bois, W.E.B. 1994. *The Souls of Black Folk*. New York: Dover Publications Inc.

Ellis, Carolyn. 1993. "'There Are Survivors': Telling a Story of Sudden Death." *Sociological Quarterly* 34 (4): 711–30.

———. 1995. *Final Negotiations: A Story of Love, Loss, and Chronic Illness*. Philadelphia, PA., USA: Temple University Press.

———. 2009. "Telling Tales on Neighbours: Ethics in Two Voices." *International Review of Qualitative Research* 2: 3–28.

Ellis, Carolyn, Tony E. Adams, and Arthur P. Bochner. 2011. "Autoethnography: An Overview." *Historical Social Research* 36 (4): 273–90.

Ellis, Carolyn, and Arthur P. Bochner. (Eds.) 1996. *Composing Ethnography: Alternative Forms of Qualitative Writing*. Lanham, MD., USA: AltaMira Press.

———. 2006. "Analyzing Analytic Autoethnography an Autopsy." *Journal of Contemporary Ethnography* 35 (4): 429–49.

Fanon, Frantz. 2008. *Black Skin White Masks*. London: Pluto Press.

Feld, Steve. 1982 *Sound and Sentiment: Birds, Weeping, Poetics, and Song in Kaluli Expression*. Philadelphia, PA., USA: University of Pennsylvania Press.

Feld, Steve, and Donald Brenneis. 2004. "Doing Anthropology in Sound." *American Ethnologist* 31 (4): 461–74.

Findlay-Walsh, Ian. 2018. "Sonic Autoethnographies: Personal Listening as Compositional Context." *Organised Sound* 23(1): 121–30.

Foucault, Michel. 1980. *Power/Knowledge: Selected Interviews and Other Writings, 1972–77*, edited by Colin Gordon. New York: Pantheon Books.

Fuss, Diana. 1989. *Essentially Speaking: Feminism, Nature & Difference*. New York and London: Routledge.

Gibson, James J. 1979. *The Ecological Approach to Visual Perception*. Boston: Houghton Mifflin.

Gidal, Marc. 2010. "Contemporary 'Latin American' Composers of Art Music in the United States: Cosmopolitans Navigating Multiculturalism and Universalism." *Latin American Music Review/Revista de Música Latinoamericana* 31 (1): 40–78.

Gilroy, Paul. 1993. *The Black Atlantic: Modernity and Double Consciousness*. London and New York: Verso.

———. 1994. "Black Cultural Politics: An Interview with Paul Gilroy by Timmy Lott." *Found Object* 4: 46–81.

———. 2001. "Black Music, Ethnicity and the Challenge of a Changing Same." In *Imagining Home: Class, Culture and Nationalism in the African Diaspora*, edited by Sidney Lemelle and Robin D. G. Kelley, 93–117. Guildford and King's Lynne: Verso.

Gilroy, Paul, and Mazal Holocaust Collection. 1991. *'There Ain't No Black in the Union Jack': The Cultural Politics of Race and Nation*. Chicago: University of Chicago Press.

Gouzouasis, Peter, and Diana Ihnatovych. 2016. "The Dissonant Duet: An Autoethnography of a Teacher-Student Relationship." *Journal of Canadian Association for Curriculum Studies* 14 (32): 14–32.

Grewal, Shabnam. 1988. *Charting the Journey: Writings by Black and Third World Women*. Sheba Feminist Publishers.

Hall, Stuart. 1990. "Cultural Identity and Diaspora." In *Identity: Community, Culture, Difference*, edited by Jonathan Rutherford, 222–37. London: Lawrence and Wishart.

Heine, Erik. 2018. "Chromatic Mediants and Narrative Context in Film." *Music Analysis* 37 (1): 103–32.

Herrmann, Andrew F. 2012. "'I Know I'm Unlovable': Desperation, Dislocation, Despair, and Discourse on the Academic Job Hunt." *Qualitative Inquiry* 18 (3): 247–55.

Hindmarsh, Jon and Alison Pilnick. 2007. "Knowing Bodies at Work: Embodiment and Ephemeral Teamwork in Anaesthesia." *Organization Studies* 28 (9): 1395–416.

Hollingworth, Lucy. 2019. "String Quartet as Autoethnography: The Writing of *Out of the Snowstorm, an Owl* (2014–17)." *Action, Criticism, and Theory for Music Education* 18 (2): 147–56.

hooks, bell. 1991. "Essentialism and Experience." *American Literary History* 3 (1): 172–83.

———. 2000. *Where We Stand: Class Matters*. New York: Routledge.

Howes, David. 2003. *Sensing Culture: Engaging the Senses in Culture and Social Theory*. Ann Arbor: University of Michigan Press.

Hung Lie, Lena Pek. 2012. "Innovation through Confrontation and Integration – Traditions of East and West in Toru Takemitsu's Art Music." *International Journal of Arts and Sciences* 5 (2): 279–89.

Hurme, Pertii, and Jukka Jouhki. 2017. "We Shape Our Tools, and Thereafter Our Tools Shape Us." *Human Technology* 13 (2): 145–8.

Hurston, Zora Neale. 2017. *Dust Tracks on a Road: An Autobiography*. New York: Harper Collins.

Hutnyk, John. 1998. "Adorno at Womad: South Asian Crossovers and the Limits of Hybridity-Talk." *Postcolonial Studies* 1 (3): 401–26.

———. 2005. "Hybridity." *Ethnic and Racial Studies* 28 (1): 79–102.

Ingold, Tim. 2000. *The Perception of the Environment: Essays on Livelihood, Dwelling and Skill*. London: Routledge.

———. 2007. *Lines: A Brief History*. Abingdon: Routledge.

———. 2008. "Against Space: Place, Movement, Knowledge." In *Boundless Worlds: An Anthropological Approach to Movement*, edited by Peter Wynn Kirby, 29–43. New York, USA and Oxford, UK: Berghahn Books.

———. 2013. *Making: Anthropology, Archaeology, Art and Architecture*. Abingdon: Routledge.

Jabavu, Noni. 1960. *Drawn in Colour: African Contrasts*. London: John Murray.

Jabbra, Nancy W. 2006. "Women, Words and War: Explaining 9/11 and Justifying U.S. Military Action in Afghanistan and Iraq." *Journal of International Women's Studies* 8 (1): 236–55.

Jessen, Edward. 2008. *Companion*. Score. Decipherer Arts Press.

John, Mary E. 1989. "Postcolonial Feminists in the Western Intellectual Field: Anthropologists and Native Informants." In *Traveling Theories, Traveling Theorists*, edited by Vivek Dhareshwar and James Clifford, Inscriptio, 49–73. Santa Cruz, CA: Group for the Critical Study of Colonial Discourse & the Center for Cultural Studies, U.C.S.C.

———. 2013. "Introduction: Coming to Know Autoethnography as More than a Method." In *Handbook of Autoethnography*, edited by Stacy Linn Holman Jones, Tony E. Adams, and Carolyn Ellis, 17–47. Walnut Creek, CA: Left Coast Press.

Jurd, Laura. 2019. *Stepping Back, Jumping In*. Album, Edition Records, UK.

Kalra, Virinder S., Raminder Kaur, and John Hutnyk. 2005. *Diaspora & Hybridity*. London: SAGE Publications Ltd.

Kalua, Fetson. 2009. "Homi Bhabha's Third Space and African Identity." *Journal of African Cultural Studies* 21 (1): 23–32.

Keddie, Nikki R. 2003. *Modern Iran: Roots and Revolution, Updated Edition*. New Haven and London: Yale University Press.

Khakpour, Porochista. 2014. "Inspiration Information: 'The Last Illusion.'" *New Yorker*.

Kisliuk, Michelle. 1997. "(Un)Doing Fieldwork: Sharing Songs, Sharing Lives." In *Shadows in the Field: New Perspectives for Fieldwork in Ethnomusicology*, edited by Gregory F. Barz and Timothy J. Cooley, 23–44. New York: Oxford University Press.

Klee, Paul. 1961. *Notebooks, Vol. 1: The Thinking Eye*, edited by Jurg Spiller. Translated by R. Manheim, London: Lund Humphries.

Knott, Kim. 2010. "Space and Movement" in *Diasporas: Concepts, Intersections, Identities*, edited by Kim Knott and Seán McLoughlin, 84–8. London and New York: Zed Books.

Krueger, Joel. 2009. "Enacting Musical Experience." *Journal of Consciousness Studies* 16 (2/3): 99–123.

LaBelle, Brandon. 2015. *Background Noise: Perspective on Sound Art*. London and New York: Bloomsbury.

Lau, Kimberley J. 2002. "This Text Which Is Not One: Dialectics of Self and Culture in Experimental Autoethnography." *Journal of Folklore Research* 39 (2/3) May–December: 243–59.

Leavy, Patricia. 2009. *Method Meets Art: Arts-based Research Practice*. New York and London: The Guilford Press.

Leedham, Christopher, and Martin Scheuregger. 2020. "The Purpose of the Written Element in Composition PhDs." In *Researching and Writing on Contemporary*

Art and Artists: Challenge, Practices, and Complexities, edited by Christopher Wiley and Ian Pace. London: Palgrave Macmillan.

Leggo, Carl. 2005. "Autobiography and Identity: Six Speculations." *Vitae Scholasticae* 22 (1): 115–33.

Leroi-Gourhan, André. 1993. *Gesture and Speech.* Translated by A. Bostock Berger. Cambridge, MA: MIT Press.

Lévi-Strauss, Claude. 1969. *The Raw and the Cooked.* New York: Harper and Row.

Lolavar, Soosan. 2014. *Only Sound Remains.* Score. Unpublished.

———. 2015. *Set Your Life on Fire.* Score. Unpublished.

———. 2016. *Girl.* Score. Unpublished.

———. 2016. *Mah Didam.* Score. Unpublished.

———. 2017. *ID, Please.* Score. Unpublished.

———. 2019. 'Golha' on *We Hope This Finds You Well In These Strange Times Vol. 2.* Album. Nonclassical.

———. 2019. 'I am the Spring, You are the Earth' on *Stepping Back, Jumping In.* Album. Edition Records.

———. 2021a. "Healing Double-Consciousness Through Creative Practice: Moving, Making and the Santoor/Self." In *Towards a Comparative Aesthetics of Music, Graz Studies in Ethnomusicology,* Vol. 27, edited by Gerd Grupe, 111–43. Herzogenrath, Germany: Shaker Verlag.

———. 2021b. "Auto-ethnography and Composition as Epistemologies for Reconciling Double-Consciousness: An Interrogation of Hybridity and Diaspora." PhD Diss. City, University of London.

———. 2022. "An Auto-Ethnographic/Compositional Approach to Questions of Diaspora and Hybridity." *Perspectives of New Music* 60 (1): 153–199.

Lolavar, Soosan and Sarah Saviet. 2023. *Every Strand of Thread and Rope.* Album. all that dust.

Lolavar, Soosan, Rosa van Hensbergen, and Kae Ishimoto. 2018. *Inventory of My Life.* 29th May 2019. Performance. City University of London, Performance Space. London.

Lorde, Audre. 2017. *Your Silence Will Not Protect You: Essays and Poems.* London, UK: Silver Press.

Maghbouleh, Neda. 2017. *The Limits of Whiteness.* Stanford, CA: Stanford University Press.

Maira, Sunaina. 1998. "Desis Reprazent : Bhangra Remix and Hip Hop in New York City." *Postcolonial Studies* 1 (3): 357–70.

Malek, Amy. 2006. "Memoir as Iranian Exile Cultural Production: A Case Study of Marjane Satrapi's Persepolis Series." *Iranian Studies* 39 (3): 353–80.

Martinez, Theresa A. 2002. "The Double-Consciousness of Du Bois & The 'Mestiza Consciousness' of Anzaldúa." *Race, Gender & Class* 9 (4): 158–76.

Mateus-Berr, Ruth, and Richard Jochum. (Eds.) 2020. *Teaching Artistic Research: Conversations Across Cultures.* Berlin, Germany: De Gruyter.

Merleau-Ponty, Maurice. 1962. *Phenomenology of Perception.* Translated by C. Smith. London: Routledge & Kegan Paul.

Moraga, Cherrie, and Gloria Anzaldúa. 1983. *This Bridge Called My Back: Writings by Radical Women of Colour.* Latham, NY: Kitchen Table Press.

Moriarty, Jess. 2013. "Leaving The Blood In." In *Contemporary British Autoethnography*, edited by Nigel P. Short, Lydia Turner and Alec Grant, 63–78. Rotterdam: SensePublishers.

Motadel, David. 2014. "Iran and the Aryan Myth." In *Perceptions of Iran: History, Myths and Nationalism from Medieval Persia to the Islamic Republic*, edited by Ali M. Ansari. London: I.B.Tauris.

Motzafi-Haller, Pnina. 1997. "Writing Birthright: On Native Anthropologists and the Politics of Representation." In *Auto/Ethnography: Rewriting the Self and the Social (Explorations in Anthropology)*, edited by Deborah Reed-Danahay, 195–222. Oxford: Berg Publishers.

Nelson, Robin. 2013. *Practice as Research in the Arts: Principles, Protocols, Pedagogies, Resistances*. Basingstoke: Palgrave Macmillan.

Nono, Luigi. 2001. "Lo Sviluppo della Tecnica Seriale" [The Development of Serial Technique]. In *Luigi Nono, Scritti e Colloqui*, edited by Angela Ida De Benedictis and Veniero Rizzardi. Milan: Ricordi.

Nooshin, Laudan. 1998. "The Song of the Nightingale: Processes of Improvisation in Dastgah Segah (Iranian Classical Music)." *British Journal of Ethnomusicology* 7: 69–116.

———. 1999. "Nightingales and Mullahs." In *World Music the Rough Guide: Africa, Europe and the Middle East*, edited by Simon Broughton, Mark Ellingham, Richard Trillo with Orla Duane, and Vanessa Dowell, 335–59. London: The Rough Guides.

———. 2014. *Iranian Classical Music: The Discourses and Practice of Creativity*. London: SOAS Musicology Series.

O'Keefe, Linda O., and Isabel Nogueira. (Eds.) 2022. *The Body in Sound, Music and Performance: Studies in Audio and Sonic Arts*. Abingdon and New York: Routledge.

Okely, Judith. 1994. "Vicarious and Sensory Knowledge of Chronology and Change: Ageing in Rural France." In *Social Experience and Anthropological Knowledge*, edited by Kirsten Hastrup and Peter Hervik. London: Routledge.

Omojola, Bode. 2007. "Black Diasporic Encounters: A Study of the Music of Fela Sowande." *Black Music Research Journal* 27 (2): 141–70.

Pace, Ian. 2016. "Composition and Performance Can Be, and Often Have Been, Research." *Tempo* 70 (275): 60–70.

Pillow, Wanda S. 2001. "Exposed Methodology: The Body as a Deconstructive Practice." *International Journal of Qualitative Studies in Education* 10 (3): 349–63.

Pink, Sarah. 2015. *Doing Sensory Ethnography*. London: Sage.

Porteous, Douglas. 1990. *Landscapes of the Mind: Worlds of Sense and Metaphor*. Toronto: University of Toronto Press.

Ramnarine, Tina K. 2007. *Musical Performance in the Diaspora*. Abingdon: Taylor & Francis.

Reed-Danahay, Deborah. 1997. *Auto/Ethnography: Rewriting the Self and the Social (Explorations in Anthropology)*. Oxford: Berg Publishers.

Reeves, Camden. 2016. "Composition, Research and Pseudo-Science: A Response to John Croft." *Tempo* 70 (275): 50–59.

Rennie, Tullis. 2016. "Composition and Identity: A Portfolio of Context-based Sound Works Following Interdisciplinary Ethnographic Methods." PhD Diss., Queens College Belfast.

Rodaway, Paul. 1994. *Sensuous Geographies: Body, Sense and Place*. London: Routledge.

Ronai, Carol Rambo. 1995. "Multiple Reflections of Child Sex Abuse: An Argument for a Layered Account." *Journal of Contemporary Ethnography* 23 (4): 395–426.

Rothstein, William. 2008. "Common-Tone Tonality in Italian Romantic Opera." *Music Theory Online* 14 (i).

Sadoh, Godwin. 2010. "The Orchestral Works of Samuel Akpabot, a Nigerian Composer-Ethnomusicologist." *The Musical Times* 151 (1913): 79–94.

Safran, William. 1991. "Diasporas in Modern Societies: Myths of Homeland and Return." *Diaspora: A Journal of Transnational Studies* 1 (1): 83–99.

Said, Edward W. 1985. "Orientalism Reconsidered." *Race & Class* 27 (2): 1–15.

———. 2003. *Orientalism*. London: Penguin.

Schaefer, Richard T. 2008. *Encyclopedia of Race, Ethnicity, and Society*. Thousand Oaks, CA: Sage Publications.

Schafer, Raymond M., et al. 1973. *The Vancouver Soundscape*. Album. Cambridge: Street Records.

Schwalgin, Susanne. 2004. "Why Locality Matters: Diaspora Consciousness and Sedentariness in the Armenian Diaspora in Greece." In *Diaspora, Identity, and Religion: New Directions in Theory and Research*, edited by Carolin Alfonso, Waltraud Kokot and Khachig Tölölyan, 72–89. London: Routledge.

Seremetakis, C. Nadia. 1994. "The Memory of the Senses: Historical Perception, Commensal Exchange, and Modernity." In *Visualising Theory*, edited by Lucien Taylor. London: Routledge.

Sharma, Ashwani. 1996. "Sounds Oriental: The (Im)Possibility of Theorizing Asian Musical Cultures." In *Dis-Orienting Rhythms: The Politics of the New Asian Dance Music*, edited by Sanjay Sharma, John Hutnyk, and Ashwani Sharma, 15–31. Atlantic Highlands, NJ: Zed Books.

Sheets-Johnstone, Maxine. 1981. "Thinking in Movement." *The Journal of Aesthetics and Art Criticism* 39 (4): 399.

Short, Nigel P., Lydia Turner, and Alec Grant. (Eds.) 2013. *Contemporary British Autoethnography*. Rotterdam: SensePublishers.

Spivak, Gayatri Chakravorty. 1988. "Can the Subaltern Speak?" In *Marxism and the Interpretation of Culture*, edited by Cary Nelson and Lawrence Grossberg, 271–313. Basingstoke: Macmillan Education.

———. 1999. *A Critique of Postcolonial Reason: Toward a History of the Vanishing Present*. Cambridge, MA: Harvard University Press.

Spry, Tami. 2001. "Performing Autoethnography: An Embodied Methodological Praxis." *Qualitative Inquiry* 7 (6): 706–32.

Stévance, Sophie, and Serge Lacasse. 2017. *Research-Creation in Music and the Arts: Towards a Collaborative Interdiscipline*. Cambridge, MA: Harvard University Press.

Stockhausen, Karlheinz. 1991. *Texte zur Musik 1984–1991 (Volume 7): Neues zu Werken vor LICHT; Zu LICHT bis MONTAG; MONTAG aus LICHT*, edited by Christoph von Blumröder. Kürten: Stockhausen Verlag.

Stokes, Martin. (Ed.) 1994. *Ethnicity, Identity and Music: The Musical Construction of Place*. Oxford; Providence, RI: Berg Publishers.

Stoller, Paul. 1989. *The Taste of Ethnographic Things: The Senses in Ethnography*. Philadelphia: University of Pennsylvania Press.

———. 1997. *Sensuous Scholarship*. Philadelphia: University of Pennsylvania Press.

Takemitsu, Asaka. 2010. *A Memoir of Tōru Takemitsu*. Bloomington, IN.: iUniverse.

Taylor, Timothy Dean. 2007. *Beyond Exoticism: Western Music and the World*. Durham, NC: Duke University Press.

Thrift, Nigel. 2006. "Space." *Theory, Culture and Society*, 23 (2–3): 139–55.

Tölölyan, Khachig. 1991. "The Nation-State and Its Others: In Lieu of a Preface." *Diaspora: A Journal of Transnational Studies* 1 (1): 3–7.

Treacher, Amal. 2000. "Welcome Home: Between Two Cultures and Two Colours." In *Hybridity and Its Discontents: Politics, Science, Culture*, edited by Avtar Brah and Annie Coombes, 96–107. London: Routledge.

Truax, Barry. 1999. *Handbook for Acoustic Ecology*. Vancouver: Cambridge Street Publishing.

Turner, Lydia. 2013. "The Evocative Autoethnographic I: The Relational Ethics of Writing About Oneself." In *Contemporary British Autoethnography*, edited by Nigel P. Short, Lydia Turner, and Alec Grant, 213–29. Rotterdam: SensePublishers.

Varahram, Farhad. 2015. *Sihayan Junub (The Black People of Iran)*. Documentary Film.

Varela, Francisco J., Evan Thompson, and Eleanor Rosch. 1991. *The Embodied Mind: Cognitive Science and Human Experience*. Cambridge, MA: MIT Press.

Varzi, Roxanne. 2008. "Miniskirt Democracy." *London Review of Books* 30 (15).

Waterston, Alisse. 2005. "Bringing the Past into the Present: Family Narratives of Holocaust, Exile, and Diaspora: The Story of My Story: An Anthropology of Violence, Dispossession, and Diaspora." *Anthropological Quarterly* 78 (1): 43–61.

Wiley, Christopher. 2019. "Autoethnography, autobiography, and creative art as academic research in music studies: A fugal ethnodrama." *Action, Criticism, and Theory for Music Education* 18 (2): 73–115.

Willis, Paul and Mats Trondman. 2002. "Manifesto for Ethnography". *Cultural Studies – Critical Methodologies* 2 (3): 394–402.

Winegar, Jessica. 2008. "The Humanity Game: Art, Islam and the War on Terror." *Anthropological Quarterly* 81 (3): 651–81.

Wolff, Janet. 1993. "On the Road Again: Metaphors of Travel in Cultural Criticism." *Cultural Studies* 7 (2): 224–39.

Xenakis, Iannis, and Sharon Kanach. (Ed.) 2008. *Music and Architecture: Architectural Projects, Texts, and Realizations*. Hillsdale, NY: Pendragon Press.

Index

Note: page numbers in *italics* indicate a figure on the corresponding page.

For Product Safety Concerns and Information please contact our EU
representative GPSR@taylorandfrancis.com
Taylor & Francis Verlag GmbH, Kaufingerstraße 24, 80331 München, Germany